How to Stay Motivated on the Deck of the Titanic

Norm Bossio

This edition published by
Dog Ear Publishing
4010 W. 86th Street, Ste H
Indianapolis, IN 46268

www.dogearpublishing.net

ISBN: 978-159858-185-0
This book is printed on acid-free paper.

Printed in the United States of America

Table of Contents

Acknowledgment

I would like to thank Kathleen Robichau, Reliable Transcription Service, Middleborough, MA for her untiring efforts, extraordinary professionalism, and incredible patience dealing with a classic Type A novice author. Without her efforts, this book would still be on my list of things to do someday.

I would also like to thank Pat O'Neill whose assistance was invaluable with printing and production issues such as page count, folios, font design, Microsoft Word, running heads, proofs, front matter, PDFs, word doc and a wide variety of other matters that far exceed my intellect, experience, and skills set.

Dedication

This book is dedicated to my Dad, Frank, whose simple life devoted to my Mom, gave me humility, a congenital hernia, a sense of humor, and a passion for everything I do.

Introduction

Having children does not come with an owner's manual. There are no extended warranties, service contracts or even directions. Other than a few biological requirements, there are no prerequisites for entering the parenting domain. Even age has loosely defined limits in terms of becoming a parent. There are, however, a gazillion books, tapes, videos, articles, and other self-help modalities to help guide parents in their lifelong quest to raise strong and healthy children. Complicating the ageless challenges of parenting include drug/alcohol abuse, violence on television, sexual exploitation in advertising, musical lyrics, high divorce rates, single parent family units, diminished social mores, and the less viable role of the church or other institutional sources for parental support. Even if the answers were available in self-help books, I suspect that the wrong parents would read them. Ask any teacher. The wrong parents attend the parent conferences. Anybody who has raised a child feels that they are an expert on parenting.

My mother gave birth to me when she was 18 years old. My Dad was 21 years old when he became my father. I remember my Mom worrying that I was not eating enough at dinnertime. Anxious that I would die of starvation, she came up with a plan. She would scream at me at the top of her lungs to eat. If this did not inspire me to finish my plate of fried liver, she would hold a solid steel pan in her left hand, place it under my chin, squeeze the nape of my neck with her right hand and threaten, "Eat, or I will kill you." I would become so upset that I would actually vomit what little I did eat into the steel pot, which was conveniently being held by my Mom under my chin. My Dad often bragged that he raised two children, Mom and me. When Mom finally brought me to the doctor because of my apparent aversion to fried liver and onions, the doctor suggested that there was nothing wrong with me that a new baby in the home would not cure. Apparently his prescription for learning how to be a parent was to just keep having children.

I recall Mom and Dad bringing me to a priest at the local parish rectory to help them discipline me. Apparently raking leaves did not work, since I always found a way to break the bamboo teeth, making the rake an impotent tool in my behavior rehabilitation program. I was so scared waiting for the priest to enter the room. When the priest finally came downstairs and sat behind his desk, I wondered what he was going to do with me. He sat, looked up at me, and took a breath to speak. Before he was able to utter a sound, I blurted out, "My Mom and Dad skip Mass every Sunday." His reaction surprised me. He started to laugh uncontrollably. I guess that behavior management strategy did not work quite as effectively as my parents had planned. Where can parents go for support, inspiration, knowledge, and direction in dealing with children? Is there a person available who might be in the best position to offer assistance in all matters related to behavior management, discipline and arbiter for all that is right and wrong? Where might such a parenting guru exist? Let us search the landscape for such a wizard.

Every child must be educated. Other than the relatively small percentage of children being home schooled, most children attend a public or private school. Education is a function of the State. For generally 180 days per year, there is a statutory requirement that each community provide a comprehensive program of instruction for kindergarten through grade 12. Each school community has a local board or committee to establish policy, administration to implement the policies, teachers, students, aides, cafeteria workers, bus drivers, office staff, nurses, custodians, parents, advisory council and a myriad of sets and subsets of constituencies with varying roles. Each school has one person responsible for the organization, administration and operation of the entire school facility. From budget planning to student discipline, one person is ultimately responsible for virtually everything that goes on in the building. Who is this teacher of teachers? Who has the background and training to know exactly what to do when the second grader's snake escapes in the cafeteria, or when the playground supervisor accidentally sits on the fifth grader's science project? Who has the experience necessary to know how to fix a jammed copy machine, to unclog a blocked toilet or to remove a crazed neighborhood dog from the auditorium during the annual spring concert? Who is this Wizard of Oz? It is, of course, the school principal. Nobody else is so uniquely qualified to inspire good, to model behavior and to fix whatever is broken. No other single person can have such an enormous impact on morale, quality of instruction, student discipline, and all matters related to the operation of the school.

Although I have not climbed Mount Everest, won an Olympic gold medal, or won a Super Bowl with a last minute field goal, I am uniquely qualified to write this book. Yes, I have been a principal in three school districts in Massachusetts. For 14 years, I served as a school principal in the towns of Walpole, Carver and Boxboro. When I was in Carver, I had the honor of being the principal of the largest public elementary school in the Commonwealth of Massachusetts. The kindergarten through grade 6 school had virtually 1,200 students in three buildings. When I was principal in Boxboro, my school had the Commonwealth's highest scores in the state- mandated testing program. I used to fly into the playground of these schools in a helicopter dressed as Santa Claus each year before the winter vacation began. I worked on and honed my "Mr. Bossio voice" during these years. I worked a total of 23 years in the public schools starting as an elementary physical education teacher and ending as a school superintendent. Being a school superintendent is much easier than serving as a building principal. Have you ever had a job that required you to wake up every school morning with a series of phone calls from various teachers (or in many cases their spouses) describing a myriad of medical symptoms justifying a sick day? I noticed that even when there was something wrong with their knees, they would be sneezing. As school principal, I had to take these calls every morning and then scramble to the substitute list to beg somebody to get up, get dressed, and spend the entire day with a class of kids who consider the day a reprieve from any semblance of a real school day. And to make this challenge even more difficult was the fact that the per diem rate would hardly pay for the gas required to get to the school. When I was a school superintendent, I actually woke up each morning with an alarm. When I was a principal, my day was sprinkled with unscheduled conferences with kids who were banished from their classes by teachers who decided to "thin the herd" for reasons ranging from a benign lack of effort to more felonious behavior such as fighting. As superintendent, I tended to meet daily with adults on more civil issues such as budget or capital improvement planning. Being a school principal was much more challenging and my most impressive credential for writing this book. Heck, anybody can win a Super Bowl by kicking a ball through uprights. I also taught third grade and served for three years as an assistant principal of a middle school. In fact, I was the first male primary grade teacher in the history of the Marshfield Public Schools. My "Mr. Bossio voice" was particularly helpful when serving as the middle school's disciplinarian for the sixth, seventh and eighth graders. If there were ever an internship to help prepare parents for managing the behavior of their children, it would be 23 years of recess duty, bus duty, cafeteria/lunchroom duty, and literally thousands of behind closed door conferences with students sent to the office bench by their harried teachers.

My formal education and preparation for the challenges of finding a garter snake in the school library includes a Bachelor of Science degree from Springfield College, a Masters of Education from Boston State College and a host of additional post-graduate work at Northeastern University. I served for 8 years as an adjunct faculty member and consultant to the management certificate program at Stonehill College.

For 17 years, I have been the sole proprietor of Norm Bossio Enterprises, a public speaking business providing technical assistance and training in a wide variety of management areas throughout the private and public sectors. Over the past several years, I have averaged over 300 speaking engagements annually. My work has carried me from British Columbia to Buenos Aires, Argentina. I have addressed more than 550 schools, colleges and universities and I have keynoted national conferences in virtually every major industry. I have spoken in front of over 2 1/2 million audience members in venues ranging from an American Indian Village Tribunal to the Hoosier Dome. I once spoke to 400 high school students, 50 lingerie salespeople, and 45 nuclear physicists all in the same day. My audiences have included a variety of notable clients such as President Bill Clinton, U.S. Supreme Court Justice Anthony Kennedy, and horror author Stephen King. In 1994, the Yankee Chapter of Meeting Planners International named me "Speaker of the Year." Finally, I have one more credential adding to my skill set and perspective as a school principal and public speaker. I am a single Dad of three grown sons. I have walked the walk. At the risk of sounding presumptuous, I feel that I can draw upon my background and experiences to address the widest range of parental concerns. I think I know why high school students are shooting each other. I have a theory of what is wrong in our schools. I have a suggestion for educational reform. I have discovered the most powerful, yet simple key to human motivation. I once spoke at a major national telecommunications call service center with the lowest employee satisfaction ratings in the entire country. The next day following my presentation, the employees' surveys soared to the highest ratings in the country. Sales in every site spiked up following my two-hour platform delivery to the sales staff. In this book, I will deal with issues of change, personality types, motivation, passion, leadership, expectations, dealing with difficult people, communication, grief, discipline, work/family balance, crisis management, stress, and simply doing good. My perspective will be unique. After all, when the copy machine jams and every primary grade teacher has toner all over her body, the parent volunteer is caught stealing the school picture money, the head custodian gives the union president the finger, and the music teacher calls in sick at noon, who do you think everyone is looking for to take charge? Thank goodness for that "Mr. Bossio voice."

Prologue

My name is Norm, and I am a single Dad of three grown sons, Andrew, Brian and Jeffrey. When my boys were young, I recall their calling me into the living room to watch a television show. I assumed that it was an educational program on public television and that they wanted to spend some quality time bonding with Dad. Naturally, it was not an educational program. It was a documentary film on roller coasters, highlighted with the highest roller coasters in the world, the most dangerous, and the best and worst maintained. The boys told me that the second highest roller coaster in the world was in Sandusky Park, Ohio, a place called Cedar Point. I knew what was coming next. "Dad, can we go to Ohio so we can ride the Magnum?" Good Dads, like good managers, do not like to say no. My experience as a school administrator occasionally slips out. Good Dads make deals. I said, "Okay, Let's draw up a contract. I will write down a few simples tasks and if you accept what I have written, sign the contract with me." Now understand that Sandusky Park is a solid two-day drive. So, I wrote up the contract. All three of my boys would have to make the honor roll for three years in a row. They would have to make their beds every day, brush their teeth, and brush each other's teeth. As luck would have it, they fulfilled their part of the contract. Dad lost the bet and we were off to Cedar Point. On a Saturday morning, we were in the driveway getting ready for the westbound trip. The four of us were in the Ford Escort settling in for a new adventure. Again, the school principalship in me sneaked out. I turned around to the boys, neatly arranged in the back seat, to make my morning announcements. "Boys, may I have your attention please?" I used the hunkiest voice I could muster. Conditions were right for the hunk voice. It was early in the morning and I did not have my coffee yet. I announced proudly, "I hope you guys know that I am not dreading this trip. I am actually looking forward to the roller coaster ride. In fact, I'm glad I lost the bet." Of course, my bragging fell on deaf ears. Brian served as the spokesperson. "Dad," he said, "We know that you are not going to really drive us to Ohio. You will wimp out. But we are going to call your bluff. We are going along with you just to keep you happy." So, we headed west on the Massachusetts Turnpike. We took pictures, stopped to souvenir hunt, ate at little diners and generally made a nice family trip of this adventure. It is strange how wonderfully alluring Indian arrowheads, tiny pocket knives and shiny cedar trinkets can look when housed in a roadside teepee guarded by an anatomically correct eight-foot moose carved out of a three ton tree trunk. Two days later, all three boys woke up from a nap just in time to see the sign on the side of the road that said, "Welcome to Ohio."

Evidently, the boys were surprised. Jeff proclaimed, "You did it Dad! You actually drove us to Ohio! We never thought you would really do this! We have been talking back here, Dad, and we have a deal for you!" I held my breath anticipating what was coming next. Jeff continued, "Dad, you don't have to ride the roller coaster. Getting us here is good enough. Let's go to a motel, go to bed early, get up early and bring us to the park. We'll ride the roller coaster. You take pictures. You're getting a little old for this." I took that statement personally. Defensively, I retorted, "Do you think that I drove to Ohio so you could ride the roller coaster? I am riding the roller coaster and I am doing so tonight!" "Awesome Dad!", they shouted. So, off we went to tame this beast.

Uneventfully, we found Cedar Point. We parked the car and we approached the Magnum. Oh my God! It was the most massive wooden structure I had ever seen. Clouds were literally covering the tops of this maze of white painted slabs of wood. A huge white sign with red letters, obviously written by an attorney looking for work, stated, "If you have any back problems, neck problems or if you are pregnant, do not board this ride. We will not assume legal responsibility for your injury or your death." There was a red line on the fence showing how tall you needed to be to get on this ride. I indeed qualified. So, the four of us joined the other 150 people in line for the ride.

Standing in line, I did my best to project an air of confidence and control. Everybody could hear the Dad from Massachusetts who lost the bet with his sons. I am certain everyone in line could hear my bragging. Frankly, I would have not only been surprised, but disappointed, if everyone did not hear my bravado. Finally, it was our turn to ride the Magnum.

Lady Luck was on my side, I think. I drew the front seat. Naturally I sat with my youngest son, Andrew (so I could protect him). Behind us sat Brian and Jeff, and behind them sat approximately 50 strangers. By now, I was bragging so loudly the whole park could have heard us. "Get this thing going," I bellowed. "I have driven a long way for this, head them up, roll them!" My boys were so proud. Three sets of hands were patting me on the back. "We are all proud of you Dad!" they pronounced. Bolstered by this spontaneous display of pride, I said, "Hey, when I say I am going to do something, I do it!"

"You are right Dad," they confirmed. Then the attendant came over. She took the stainless steel safety bar, pulled it over us and flicked some sort of latch contraption on the side. With the ominous metal-to-metal click, a strange thing happened to me. I died! My heart started to pound. My face flushed red. Hives appeared on my neck, chest and back. I was shocked from the sudden change from unbridled confidence to untold terror. Why? I was not nervous throughout the entire trip. I was so cool and calm in line, settling into the little roller coaster seat and right up until the safety belt flattened my shoulders and thighs into the seats. What changed? Then I realized what had happened. I lost control. I could have called the trip off. I could have stepped out of line. I could have pulled a U-turn at any time during the trip. I had lots of options right up to one moment, the click. Once I heard that click, all my options were gone. A little voice in my head said, "Norm, you are going for a ride." At that instant, I whipped my head around and frantically yelled, "God, get me out of this thing! There is no way I am going to ride this!" It was too late. The cart jerked forward. My neck was pulled backwards from the thrust of the chain under us. We were headed straight up into the air. My face was getting jerked in unison with the chain. All I could see was the sky. I was grabbing the bar for dear life. Of course, my sons were waving their arms frantically over their heads shouting, "Like this Dad! Like this!" I yelled at my kids to hold onto the bar. I may have used a few extra adjectives. I am now the only person you could hear throughout the entire park. The reason was simple. I was worried about my kids, until we reached the top. At that point, I did not give a damn about my kids.

Down we roared. My stomach seemed to rest in my head. All I really remember doing was swearing. I used every swear that I could ever remember. I recalled some old ones from Junior High School. I actually made dirty words up. If it sounded dirty, I yelled it out! Finally, the ride was over. My son said, "Dad, where did you hear those words?" The bar came up. I stepped out onto wobbly legs. Desperately, I tried to regain my composure. I am Dad. I am in charge. I need to look like I am in control. So I mustered up whatever dignity I had left and I attempted to walk away. At that moment, I realized my stomach had become nauseous. My face had blanched white. I was hunched forward at the hips temporarily, I hoped. Jeff held me up by one armpit, while Brian held me up by the other one. So, with all the control and dignity of an adult, I slinked away. We walked back towards the line of 150 people waiting in line for their turn to ride the Magnum. At that very moment, we passed by the front of this line (in clear view of everyone). Andy ran up in front of me, looked up at my face and yelled loudly enough so that everyone could hear him, "Hey Dad! You gonna throw up?" Of course, this is all I needed to hear. It pushed me over the edge. The only thing worse than throwing up is throwing up in front of an audience. It was disgusting. Helplessly, I bent over to project untold stomach contents all over the hot top, splattering onto my boys' new sneakers. I could not tell whether the audience was gasping in horror or laughing in disbelief. I do, however, know that everyone was looking. The boys were quite amused as they gleefully shouted, "Awesome, Dad, awesome!" I went from leader of the pack to a humiliated victim of his own bravado. After several moments of this humiliation, I recovered enough of my composure to get back in line for three more rides. Why? What would make me return to the terror that minutes before humbled me as the leader of the pack? Did I enjoy the pain? Was I trying to prove something? Am I a sick man?

This book is going to address many of these kinds of questions. I will explore and discuss the many frustrations, stressors and opportunities facing all of us daily. Clearly, this book will not serve as a class text in any undergraduate, graduate or certificate program in management, yet many management issues will be addressed. One will recognize concepts of time, stress, crisis and change management. Communication skills, team building, motivation, decision-making, problem solving and strategic planning will be discussed anecdotally, but not conceptually. A review of the literature, charts, graphs and statistical data will be noticed only by their absence. I will not be listing habits of successful people primarily because I would be afraid that I would be missing too many of them. I will not be quoting the management gurus, McGregor, Maslow, Lippit, Pareto or Hershberg. If you have already thumbed through the pages ahead of you, you may have noticed that there are no footnotes. I never quite mastered the difference among Ibid., Op. cit., and et al. Once I realized those were Latin terms, my attention span waned. My roots go deep in this regard since I took two years of Latin I with Mrs. Gutterson at Braintree High School. Mrs. Gutterson is also the same teacher who told my mother at a parent conference that I was not "college material." Hence, you will not find footnotes in this book. Perhaps this roller coaster ride is a metaphor for all of us trying to balance work and family. The ups and downs of parenting, working and just plain living will sound very familiar. There are no jokes in this book. I tell jokes poorly. I can only imagine how poorly I would write them. So, why do I enjoy roller coaster rides so much? What is it about my personality that thrives on adventure? Perhaps the word adventure is a self-serving substitute for crisis. Since my formal training in college was in the field of education, administration and management, I am sure I have all the tools necessary to manage my life. Then why am I constantly feeling like I am playing catch-up? Why do I feel like I never have enough time to do the things I want to do? I have spent a lifetime trying to find the answer. I am at the stage of my life when I am beginning to consider the possibility (however remote), the simple, but eloquent question. Am I the problem?

Chapter 1: Do People Change?

The issue of change in a person's life is often associated with stress, anxiety and turmoil. Stress is simply how a person responds to a certain situation. An argument can be made that all change results in stress. Stress is not necessarily a bad thing. The opposite of love is not hate, it is indifference. People who are indifferent do not worry about anything. Ironically, they seem to live forever. It would seem that the price we pay for passion is the resultant stress. The only things that seem to drive us crazy are things that are important. Perhaps this is why parents worry about their children forever.

Ask a bride and groom if they are worried about their wedding. If they admit that their upcoming wedding is stressful, suggest that they cancel it. Getting married can be equally as stressful as getting divorced. Christmas can be stressful. Vacations can be stressful. Losing a job is stressful. Interviewing for a new job can be equally stressful. Winning a lottery can be stressful, although I suppose that stress might be worth the risks. It is fair to say that all changes are stressful. There are no distinctions between good stress and bad stress, at least as far as our bodies are concerned. Our hearts pump faster, blood pressure increases, blood flow changes directions and breathing becomes more rapid. Our bodies respond in a similar fashion to stress of any kind. A young child responds to his dropped ice cream cone in much the same way as an adult responds to the tragic news that a best friend has been critically injured. The sense of loss, the tears and the pain are at least in relevant terms virtually the same.   While the consequences of the losses are obviously disparate, the initial physiological responses are identical.

Perhaps it would be useful to look at the nature of change. By doing so, it may be easier to manage the process of change in our lives. Since ongoing change is not going to go away, let us try to begin to understand it. If we learn to manage change, maybe stress will be minimized and we can devote our energies to more effective survival strategies and coping mechanisms.

Do people change? Of course people change. Who would want to fly in an airplane before the pilot gets his or her license? Can you imagine having surgery with a person who was really very nice, but never quite made it through high school? I would prefer sitting in the back of a large commercial aircraft where the pilot has gray hair and many hours of flying experience. I am not sure about others, but I would prefer that my surgeon graduate from medical school. People change all the time. At the very least, we should accept that people are capable of change. Otherwise, why would we go to schools, to conferences or to meetings? If people do not change, why would we be on this earth more than one day? People join health clubs, find support groups, make New Year's resolutions, start dating again, break up with old relationships, stop smoking, lose weight and stop drinking. I lost 54 lbs. in six months. I did not need any particular diet. I have little league games to make up and school concerts to attend. I may or may not have been the perfect Daddy. I am, however, the perfect Grampa. I used to go to Dunkin Donuts every morning to order a large cup of coffee with extra cream and sugar, a heated coffee roll and if I felt particularly religious that day, I would add a vanilla angel doughnut for the road. Now I get a medium black coffee, no sugar with a toasted wheat bagel, no cream cheese. Yes, people are capable of change.

Do we change others? Of course we do not change others. I call that the "rescue fantasy." People change themselves. From time to time, I am introduced as the "Motivational speaker from Massachusetts." I immediately correct the well-meaning host by saying that I am not the "Motivational speaker from Massachusetts." I am, however, the "Motivated speaker from Massachusetts." There is a big difference. I do not motivate. I do not change others. I motivate one person in this world. I motivate me. One of the nice things about being motivated is that it spreads. One of the sad things about being miserable is that it also spreads. That is why every group of people has miserable people who clump together. Typically, the miserable people meet together for lunch. They enjoy their downtime by being miserable. Listen carefully, eating lunch. Ever hear the words, "This place sucks!" being uttered in the lunchroom? Miserable people also enjoy meeting in the parking lot by their cars before going home. Rather than go home and enjoy their family or free time, many would prefer to stay in the parking lot and complain about the day. Motivation comes from the Latin word motivere. Motivere means "from within." Motivation literally means from inside. We do not change other people.

I was a teacher, a principal and a school superintendent in Massachusetts Public Schools for 23 years. When I was a school principal in a neighborhood public elementary school, I once had a little boy sent to my office for swearing. According to the teacher, the 7-year-old second grader used the "F" word. Now let me tell you that is big time for a 7-year-old second grader! He said that he used that word in the cafeteria in front of 200 children, 10 teachers and 3 parent volunteers. I gasped theatrically. I was appalled. I threatened to keep him in the second grade until he was 18 years old, indoor recess for the rest of his life and I was going to call his Godparents. His lower lip pouted, his head fell forward and he started to cry. My heart broke. I felt terrible. Have you ever worried about somebody else's safety even more than they do or concern yourself with another person's future? As an educator, I have actually caught myself worrying about a child apparently more than his own parents! Clearly, I am a slushball. Making this little boy cry made me feel awful, despite his use of the dreaded "F" word in the school cafeteria.

So, I made a deal with the little boy. If he promised to never swear again in my school so that anybody could hear him (I figured that would be safe enough), I would give him one more chance. We shook hands and sealed the deal. Did I see him again? Oh, yes. That afternoon, the teacher had him by the nape of the neck, marched him into my office and announced, "He swore again!" However, this time the teacher was not just angry with the lad. This time she was angry with me. I could not fix him! Nobody fixes anybody else. We only fix ourselves and only if we really desire the change. Sadly, slushballs actually assume responsibility for the behavior (or misbehavior) of others. Occasionally, we get in trouble when other people mess up. Life would be simpler if we started with the assumption that we are the only people we can change and that assuming responsibility or blame for the behavior of others is not only unfair, but it is also unwarranted.

Do people resist change? At first blush, it would seem that we crave stability, continuity and routine. Change can be threatening to the notion of predictability. I have, however, a different perspective on the notion of resistance to change. If somebody offers you an additional $500.00 on your next payroll check, what would you say? What if the additional money had no strings attached to it? There would be no addition to your job description and you would never have to pay back the money. Would you refuse the additional money because it would change the amount of money you would be receiving? Would you prefer to receive the usual amount? In all likelihood, you would jump at the chance to receive the additional cash. Would you prefer the stability, continuity and routine of receiving a lesser amount? Perhaps the key here is how the change is perceived to affect us. When purchasing a new automobile, listen to what the salesperson says. Would the salesperson say, "Please buy this car. I need the commission." or would you more likely hear, "This car seems perfect for you. Maybe you should purchase this car." I have recently lost a lot of weight. I did so for me. I had some cosmetic dental work done so that I would look better. I use seatbelts, not because it is law, but because I have too many little league games, school plays, weddings, graduations and so forth to attend. An argument can be made that volunteers are selfish people. It makes them feel so good when they give their time to help others. All change is perceived in personal terms. We are far more likely to readily accept change if it is perceived to be good for us. We tend to vote for people whose views are similar to our own. We tend to surround ourselves with people who are similar to us. As a result, we often see cliques at work, neighborhood alliances and even family collaborations.

The worst form of change is mandated. "Do it this way because I said so." "You are required by law, statutory requirement, federal mandate, past practice or written policy." or "I am your father." are all compelling reasons to behave in certain ways, but not necessarily an effective way to assure compliance. We all know the urban legend of the parent forbidding a son or daughter to date "that person." The parent forbids ever talking with the pariah. Despite the dictates, the parent later discovers that not only are they dating, but they are setting a wedding date and are in the final steps of picking a name for the new baby.

What kind of feedback encourages change? When my sons were younger, they always wanted a puppy. I did not want to get one. Since I am the Dad, I am in charge and I am the boss, I simply said, "No dog in this house!" Of course, my sons asked the inevitable question, "Why not?" Because they were so young, my response was simple, "Because I said so!" They accepted my answer without further discussion. Those were simpler times. As we all know, children get older and taller. Several years later, my sons informed me that they were older now and they would like to get a new puppy. However, I am still the boss and I am still in charge. My response was the same, "No, we are not getting a dog!" Despite my using my best Mr. Bossio principal voice and tone, they asked the inevitable question, "Why not Dad?" This gets so complicated. Now, I have to come up with an articulate reason. I need to find a specific and rational response. Picking my words carefully, I responded, "I am at work all day. You boys are in school all day. What are we going to do with a puppy during the day? Do we tie him up to a tree? What if the puppy wraps himself around the tree and the rope tightens around his neck? Dogs (and humans) have carotid arteries on either side of their neck. Cutting off the blood supply to the brain with the rope will result in a dead puppy at the base of the tree when we came home! Is this fair to the puppy?" Horrified with the visual I just painted in their minds, the boys said, "No way, Dad, that would be awful!" So far, I am doing well resisting the inevitable. We all know what children do. They grow older, get taller and they just wear us down!

The day finally came when they surrounded me, looked down at me and said, "Dad, we are getting a dog!" I looked up and said, "Okay, fine, we will get one." Now I have a problem. How do I get my sons to accept responsibility and take care of the dog without a major crisis at the Bossio residence? Well, let us review what we already know about managing change. Are my sons capable of change? Yes, my sons are absolutely capable of change. Will I be able to change them? No, ultimately they will be changing themselves. Will they resist change? No, my sons will not resist change if they perceive the change to be in their best interest. My challenge was clear.

In all my graduate classes in management, I was taught how important it is to get people involved in decision-making and to empower people to participate in the process and establish collaborative approaches to group problem solving activities.

A "bottoms up" model of institutional decision-making will ultimately be more effective in terms of managing change. If this model works so well in corporate America, it should work well in the Bossio household. I also learned that if this model of managing change is done correctly, the people involved will actually think that the change was their idea. The notion of "total quality management" was based on many of these organizational assumptions. So, here is the plan. I will let my three sons name the dog. If they name the dog, they would assume more responsibility for the dog and eventually take better care of the pup. Delegating is always risky. I learned in my Masters program that when managers delegate, they only delegate authority, not responsibility. Managers cannot delegate responsibility. If a subordinate makes a mistake on a task delegated by a manager, it is the manager who is ultimately responsible.

As an elementary principal, my favorite part of the day was bus dismissal. It was so fun to stand in front of the school exchanging goodbyes with the children and complimenting them on their new shoes, fresh haircut, art projects or test papers with stickers for good work. The children were also more careful approaching and boarding the school buses when Mr. Bossio was around. It also provided a good excuse for me to get out of my office into the fresh air. There was something particularly satisfying for me to observe school buses fill up with the children. Watching the buses leave, as I wave to the kids, seemed to bring a nice closure to the day. One day, I was out of town and obviously unable to do my usual bus dismissal. I asked another staff member if she were available to fill in for me in my absence. When people have tasks delegated to them, they have the option of saying no, because as a rule the task being delegated to them is not generally on their job description. If it were, it would be insubordinate to say no. In a sense, I was asking the teacher to do a piece of my job in my absence. She graciously agreed to do so without any reservation. Now remember, she had not done bus duty in the past. Unfortunately, she messed up big time. She forgot to dismiss the entire 5th and 6th grades. Virtually 100 children missed the buses. Apparently when the children realized the school buses left without them, they went nuts. They left their classes in any way they could, through locked doors, fire exits, windows and the front lobby door to chase the buses down main street. When the parents realized that they were greeting buses one-third empty, they went nuts. They called the school and the police, and they started looking for their missing children. From what I learned later, the entire school community was a veritable zoo.

When I returned to school the next day, who was in trouble? The answer is obvious. Clearly I was the person who was being held responsible and accountable for the mishap that occurred the day before, and rightfully so. Despite the fact that I was not around for the bus dismissal miscues, I was in trouble because a manager can never delegate responsibility. I only delegated the authority to do bus duty (as a favor to me). Thank goodness no child was hurt or missing for very long. The manager always maintains the responsibility for tasks delegated to others. Interestingly enough, one would assume that managers would tend to delegate to responsible people. Unfortunately, however, they do not. Managers tend to delegate to subordinates who tend to say yes. No manager is going to seek out a subordinate who is going to respond, "Where does it say in my job description that I am supposed to be doing this for you?" We do the same thing at home with our own children. If we wearily come home after a long day at work, plop ourselves down in our favorite chair, take off our shoes, close our eyes, and settle into the comfort of our own space, what do we do when we would like one of our children to bring us a glass of water? Let us consider the options available to us. What if we look across the room and see two of our children sitting on either side of the couch? On one end of the couch is the younger child, who is obviously happy to see you home and is making every effort to make you feel welcome. On the other end of the couch, is your older adolescent wearing a headset, rap music blaring in his ears, and is virtually unaware that you are home, let alone in the same room. Which child are you going to ask to get your glass of water? My guess is that you are going to avoid asking the adolescent. It would be much easier to ask the young child who appeared more eager to please you. In a sense, this is how many managers delegate. Perhaps this is why in many office settings where there are two people, the two personalities could not be more different. Have you ever noticed that one secretary is usually an absolutely lovely saint, while the other one is often the most miserable SOB to ever walk the earth? At the risk of appearing contentious here, which secretary would you ask to stay late to help you catch up on some clerical tasks that you have ignored or procrastinated? This hardly seems fair, but as we know, life is not always fair. My best teachers seemed to have the most challenging students in their classes.

Having said all of this, I am going to take the leap of faith and delegate the authority to my three sons to name the dog. Knowing the risks associated with delegation, it will be worth it to me if doing so results in the boys being more responsive, attentive, and responsible for the dog. My sons will love naming the dog. It is now time to implement my strategic plan.

Chapter 2: They Named Her Shemp

We went off to the mall to buy a puppy. After some debate, we came to consensus on a gorgeous little Golden Retriever. Golden Retrievers have very pleasant temperaments. I am convinced that you could do anything to a Golden. You can pull their tails. I think they kind of enjoy it. You can ride them around the house like a little horse. They do not mind if you roll them over on their backs and tickle them. I paid $400.00 for this little purebred. What the heck, I put it on my credit card. Twenty-eight percent over 30 years, who's going to care? So, now is the time to delegate the authority to the boys to name the dog.

That night, I prayed. I reminded God that I hardly ever asked for favors. I thanked Him often for the many blessings I have. However, tonight I was departing from this history of past practice. I needed a favor. I was going to let my sons name this dog without any input from me. I was going to have to live with whatever name they chose. I asked for divine intervention. "Please aim my sons towards a name that is consistent with the $400.00 that I paid for the damned thing!" God did not listen. They named her Shemp. I was so disappointed. They named this beautiful little puppy after one of the Three Stooges. Nobody watches the Three Stooges, unless you are under the age of 10 or, of course, male. However, I wrote Shemp on the AKC registration papers. Indeed, the risks of delegation were obvious. However, with any luck at all, my boys would take responsibility to take care of the dog, because, after all, they named her.

The first night, we were all sitting in the living room, Jeffrey, Brian, Andrew, Dad and Shemp. Unfortunately, Shemp did a bad thing. She left a little treat on the carpet. I looked at my sons with the "What are you going to do now?" look on my face. My sons scattered. Left alone with Shemp and her gift on the carpet, I planned my first response. I recalled reading somewhere that if you rub the dog's nose in it, she will quickly become housebroken. Now that is a motivational technique! So, I did exactly that; rubbing her nose in the mess, I used my "Mr. Bossio Principal voice again" and said, "Bad Shemp, bad dog!" I then put her outside immediately. Obviously for Shemp, this was negative feedback. The next day, the same scenario emerged, Jeffrey, Brian, Andrew, Dad and Shemp in the living room. This time, a good news/bad news dilemma occurred. Good news: Shemp did not leave her treat on the living room carpet. Bad news: This time she left her gift in the kitchen. Again, my boys scattered to places unknown, leaving me to deal with the emerging pattern of Shemp's problematic behavior. Again, I introduced Shemp's nose to her kitchen floor deposit and shouted, "Bad Shemp!" Her ears were pinned backwards, her tail was tucked between her legs and she was trembling pathetically. Again, I provided negative feedback for this little puppy. On the third day, I was playing touch football outside with my boys, their friends, and of course Shemp. In the middle of game I saw what I thought was the most beautiful sight I had ever seen. Shemp was doing it again, but this time outside. It was awesome! I did not want to interrupt this magical moment, so I yelled out, "Freeze!" So, all the humans froze watching Shemp complete the task. When she finished, we all ran over and hugged Shemp and gave her accolades, "Good dog! Good Girl! Yay Shemp!" Andy ran into the house to get a little biscuit treat for her. We all celebrated. Shemp's tail was wagging in delight. If dogs had lips, Shemp would be smiling. In any case, it was obvious she was enjoying our attempts to reward her behavior. This time, Shemp was receiving positive feedback.

Forgive me for using a dog as my analogy; however, it appears to me that the only feedback that inspires change is negative feedback. However, we must catch people doing things right. The strongest motivational technique is a sincere and well-deserved, "Thank you, Well Done! and Nice Job!" A pat on the back works wonderfully to sustain desired behavior. People work for money. People work hard for recognition and appreciation. Perhaps we should not wait for a heart attack to begin to lose weight. Maybe we should work on nurturing relationships before the divorce. Maybe the time to forgive our parents is before they die. The things we tend to worry about are not the things that change our lives. Our lives change with the things we least expect. A telephone call in the middle of the night from an emergency room in a hospital would change our lives forever. A blood test, a lump on our breast, a prostate test or a drunk driver can change our lives. I am choosing not to waste one day.

Gratitude, appreciation and a thank you cost nothing, except the modest effort necessary to recognize and to value others.

Chapter 3: Trade School's King of Swat

Everybody loves my Dad. One of ten children to two Italian immigrants, Raphael and Guiseppe, Francis Dominic Bossio was the smartest, most humble, best baseball player I have ever known. He could do anything. He could build tree houses, add breezeways, frame porches, grow huge tomatoes, draw perfect Donald Ducks, float on his back with both feet sticking out of the water, give up smoking, play ping pong, win newspaper contests ($1,000.00 for second place in the old Record American "Who's your pick in 56?" election contest), make a baseball actually curve, hit any fastball and stay married until death did him part. Boston Trade School named him King of Swat because of his extraordinary accomplishments in high school. He was the school's best pitcher, best outfielder and had one of the highest batting averages in the Boston High School league. He threw right-handed, but batted from the left side of the plate. My oldest son, Jeffrey, does the same. His high school yearbook documented his legendary feats.

"When he's on the plate, things get hot.
He will put an opponent on the spot.
What's he got that we have not?
Why he is Trade School's King of Swat."

Dad always said that nobody could ever strike him out. To my knowledge, nobody ever did. I remember many times having Dad at two strikes before he belted the Wiffle ball clean over to our neighbor's house across the street (the Conn's). I was so disappointed then. Looking back, I am so glad.

I was never a very good baseball player. I recall Dad watching me play on the East Braintree's Little League Team called the "Penguins." He would sit there and watch me in my orange shirt strike out over and over again. I was only 9 years old, yet I sensed his gentle encouragement, but subtle disappointment. When I was in high school, I played Babe Ruth League baseball. I was an average player. I never really hit for power, but I had a good arm and I was a very fast runner. Nevertheless, I was never in my Dad's league. I really liked the dark blue flannel Babe Ruth League Eagles uniforms with the stretched blue stockings pulled up to my knees. My biggest disappointment was the afternoon I hit a home run at Hollis Field. My Dad missed the game. When I was older, we played in various softball leagues. Dad even formed a neighborhood team called, "The Birchcroft Bombers" and we would play softball games on Sunday mornings. He worked in the Post Office as a postal mechanic fixing and installing mailboxes. He would receive an annual safety pin for his "year of unreported accidents" driving the mail truck. Dad would wink every time he used the word "unreported." The Post Office had a Sunday morning softball team. Dad pitched, while I played left field. After Sunday Mass, Dad and I would play league softball games in a variety of locations throughout the Greater Boston area. While my father's throwing and fielding skills were diminishing, he could always hit the ball anytime, anywhere, and anyplace he wished. As a result, pitching was the perfect position for him to play. I recall one warm summer evening, we had a softball game under the lights in a little field in Quincy. The field may have been about 15 miles from my Dad's house in Braintree. For some reason, the coach chose not to let my Dad start the game. Frank was crushed. He sat in the bleachers (not on the bench) with his glove tucked under his arm. My Dad wanted to pitch. I felt so badly for him.

Sometime during the game, I hit a home run over the left field fence. As I was rounding second base, I looked up to see my Dad. He was gone. My first reaction was the selfish notion that he missed another one of my home runs. However, it then occurred to me that he was missing. I jumped in my car to find him. I found him approaching Quincy Center, walking the 15 miles home to Braintree. I learned that night that even a King of Swat can have his heart broken.

Chapter 4: The Price for Speaking Italian

Mom was more intense than my Dad. Ruth was the only child born to Norman and Ruth McGillivray. She was a stubborn blue-eyed Irish child. When Ruth's Dad was in the Navy, her Mom died of tuberculosis. This left Mom to bounce around living with various relatives. At 16, Mom got written permission from her Dad to marry a 19 year-old Italian/American named Frank. Back in those days, the Irish and Italians never talked to each other. Those two married. I am the sole result of that union. I have no brothers or sisters.

Mom was the driving force behind us. Her survival skills and strong sense of independence served us well. While my grandmother (my Dad's Mom) was crushed that he was marrying an Irish woman who obviously could not make Italian meatballs, it was ironic that it was Mom's extraordinary ability to survive that inspired both Dad and me. We lived upstairs in a small apartment in Brighton, MA. I recall sitting in front of an open oven in the kitchen to stay warm during the winter months. One day, when I was quite small, I came home after playing downstairs with my little Italian preschool friends. Little did I know that the moment I opened my mouth, our futures would change dramatically. I was speaking Italian.

My mother almost died right there in front of me. At that moment, Mom decided that she wanted to move away and buy a house. No child of hers was going to grow up in a Boston suburb speaking Italian.

Dad responded by challenging my Mom to come up with $1,000.00. If she did, they would buy a house. Five years later, Ruth showed Frank $1,000.00 in cash. Shortly thereafter, we moved to Braintree, Massachusetts into a small ranch in a quiet post-war development neighborhood. I recall having everything I ever needed. Both Mom and Dad worked and they saved for the day that I would be going to college. Mom was a saver. She was extraordinarily tight with a dollar. Dad could not buy new cars, yet I always had new school clothes every September. I recall wonderful Christmases. My parents adored each other. Being an only child, I certainly was the center of my parents' universe. Mom burned her maternity clothes after giving birth to me. Mom had a sense of humor, but she was more measured as to when she would use it. One Halloween, as Dad was answering the door giving out the goodies to the neighborhood children as they were trick or treating, Mom decided to have some fun. As the night progressed and there were fewer and fewer children at the door, Mom disappeared for several minutes. The doorbell rang and Dad dutifully answered the door. Standing at the door was a witch in full costume including a very graphic latex mask. As Dad reached to get some candy, the witch pulled up her black full-length costume dress and yelled, "Trick or Treat!" Of course, this witch had obviously nothing on under the costume. Thank God I was not in the room to observe this special holiday treat! This witch was, of course, my Mom. My Dad screamed. He invited the witch in since his wife was "out of town for the evening." He insisted that he did not recognize her naked body. That story became a Halloween holiday legend as the years passed.

Mom was the fire in my belly. She taught me independence, self-direction and focus. She was a strict disciplinarian. My Dad often said that he raised two children, Mom and me. Somehow, I feel in my heart that it was my mother who made me an overachiever. She was a hard worker and taught me the value of determination. She was a survivor. She would accept nothing less than 100% effort in everything that I did. After I graduated from college, Mom was diagnosed with Parkinson's disease. She was now facing the challenge of her life to remain determined, despite her failing body.

Chapter 5: Parents Are Supposed To Live Forever

Dad had a cough that did not seem to go away. His consistent dry cough did not respond to the typical over-the-counter medicines. He coughed so much that he actually got a double inguinal hernia. In preparation for the double hernia operation, Dad had x-rays taken of his lungs to see why he was coughing so much. An unexplained spot was noted that required further investigation. At the hospital, Dad's double hernia was fixed. It was, of course, routine and successful. However, the surgeon also opened up Dad's chest to investigate the spot on his lung. Once the lung was exposed, it was clear that Dad's double hernia was the least of his problems.

When Dad was in the Navy, he was assigned to the shipyard. His job was simple. Somebody ordered Frank to line the walls of the ship with rolls of insulation material. He was taught by his mother and the Navy to simply comply with a snappy, "Yes Sir!" Apparently the material was good for ship hulls, but bad for human lungs. The material was, of course, asbestos. After so many years, the asbestos had turned into a fast spreading form of cancer, mesothelioma. Since the cancer was more liquid, rather than mass in nature, radiation or chemotherapy were not very effective treatment options. It was simply going to be a matter of time for my Dad. After several days in the hospital recovering from the hernia surgery and the exploratory lung procedure, Dad was allowed to go home.

Mom was not doing particularly well. Her Parkinson's disease was progressing to the point whereby she had limited mobility, reduced strength and difficulty speaking. She would not allow the visiting nurses to visit Dad at home. I went to help my Mom with Dad. Mom had little physical or emotional energy to really help him. I slept next to Dad, while Mom slept alone in my old room. When it was time for hospice, Mom would not let them in the door. She insisted on taking care of Dad without help from anybody, except me. Dad was failing fast. It was time for me to take Dad to Quincy City Hospital. He was losing weight and his pain medication was becoming less and less effective. Clearly, Mom and I were not going to be able to continue taking care of Dad at home. I recall Dad asking me what it was going to be like to die. He wondered if he was going to choke or simply feel like he was falling asleep. I wanted so badly for Mom to let Dad talk to somebody from hospice. She was so stubborn.

The day finally came when it was time to drive Dad to the hospital. Mom stayed home. I backed my car out of the driveway and drove Dad from his home in Braintree to Admitting at Quincy City Hospital. Not a word was spoken. We both knew that he would not see his house again. His eyes were sad. His long thin fingers were folded in his lap. His seat was set back to relieve the pain he was feeling throughout his frail body. He sat in silence. After driving about halfway to the hospital, Dad turned to me and said, "I'm sorry." I never asked him what he was sorry for. I figured it was not important at this point. I simply told him that it was okay.

Dad was now checked into the hospital. After several days of rest, taking visitors, and saying goodbyes, it was obvious that Dad was failing quickly. I specifically recall the last time Andy visited Dad at the hospital. It seemed so final, so simple, so unfair that his last words to Andy were a benign, "Come here. Give me one more hug!" After several days in the hospital, Dad asked me if I would visit him after work. "Of course," I said. I would be happy to visit him that night. I informed him that it might be real late because I had three speaking engagements scheduled for that day. The last speech was an after dinner speech at a restaurant in Northampton, MA. That speech may run late (dinner speeches usually do), and

Northampton was at least a three-hour drive to Quincy City Hospital. Dad asked me to come no matter how late it was. I assured him that I would do so.

Dinner speeches can be particularly frustrating because nobody can control how timely the food is served, how quickly it is eaten, and how expeditiously the tables are cleared. Dinner speeches often run painfully late. I joke that I make a living waiting for people to finish eating. This speech was not going to be an exception. The dinner went on forever. Originally I was scheduled to speak around 8:00 p.m. On this night, however, I was not introduced until almost 10:00 p.m. I finished speaking at 11:00 p.m. to a standing ovation. While the audience's response was exhilarating, I was dreading the long drive home to visit my Dad at the hospital. I finally started my drive to the hospital at approximately 11:15 p.m.

I recall how tired I was. I struggled to keep my eyes open. I opened the car windows and turned up the radio just to keep awake. I began to rationalize about driving home, getting a good night's sleep, and visiting Dad early the next morning. I figured a nice shower would make me a more hospitable visitor, particularly if I brought a newspaper and a fresh cup of coffee for Dad and me. I'm sure that Dad would not mind the slight change of plans.

Now came the late night moment of truth. Should I turn off Route 95 South to my home in Lakeville, or continue to Quincy to visit my Dad? It was almost 2:00 a.m. and I could not turn the wheel to go home. I was going to visit Dad. He better appreciate this! I was really exhausted. I did not want to do this.

I parked my car in the mostly empty parking lot of the hospital. I slammed the door, grabbed my parking ticket and entered the hospital lobby. I took the elevator to Dad's floor and walked to his room. As I pushed the door open, I saw my Dad sitting up in his light blue hospital pajamas. He glowed as he blurted out, "You did come tonight! Thank you!" I responded with an almost reticent, "Of course I came Dad, I promised I would, remember?" We chatted briefly about unimportant things. He said that he was actually feeling much better and that he had a wonderful day. I was relieved to see that Dad was in such good spirits.

After talking for about 30 minutes, I asked Dad if I could stay and sleep in his room. I told him I had a long day and that I was really very tired. He said I could and he pointed to a large leather chair at the end of his bed. He said to take my suit jacket off and to sleep there. The chair looked so good to me. I lay down in the chair, said goodnight to Dad and he thanked me for visiting him. I said that he was perfectly welcome and that I loved him. I woke up the next morning. He did not. Imagine if I went home so I could get a good night's sleep. Aren't Dads supposed to live forever?

Chapter 6: Type A's and Type B's

A review of the classic literature would suggest that personality types can be differentiated and discussed in many ways. Many authors, researchers and theorists have attempted to categorize personality types by virtue of behaviors and temperaments. While I certainly respect, indeed admire the myriad of personality inventories, surveys and questionnaires generated to measure personalities using quantifiable measurements, I will take a more simplistic anecdotal approach. Not knowing where to start, let me take Julie Andrews' lyrical suggestion in the Sound of Music and start at the beginning. Where better to start than with Type A's and Type B's?

Type A's

Type A's are often called "hyper." They tend to be impatient and driven. Watch people at airports on escalators. Type A's do not stand on escalators going up. They walk up the steps as the escalator moves upwards. Just think how great that is, double time to the next level! Type A's have to wait for automatic doors to open up. If you live with a Type A, they probably spend their time raking leaves, organizing closets or making certain that all cans have labels facing forward in the cabinets. Watch young children draw pictures. Intently, they concentrate on making the picture just the way they want it. If the child makes a mistake, notice the frustration as the toddler crumples the paper up, throws it away and begins another picture. Watch out for these children. They tend to become perfectionists. Perfectionism is a terrible motivator. The next time your child comes home with a report card that has all A's and B's on it, and one C, listen to the first sentence out of your mouth. If the first sentence includes the letter C in it, do not be surprised if she becomes anorexic at 16 or bulimic at 18, as this beautiful child seeks the perfect body to match her perfect picture and perfect report card. Type A's have no problem using "Wite Out" when they make an error on a piece of paper. Their problem is in waiting for the "Wite Out" to dry before writing on it. Type A's smudge and curse a lot. Type A's love to be busy. They often confuse being busy with being productive. Type A's often have difficulty managing their time because they are too busy doing lots of things that are not important. They tend to be efficient, but not effective. Efficient people take care of urgent matters (putting out recurring fires), while effective people address matters that make a difference (figuring out why the fires are starting). Type A's occasionally find it more satisfying just to remain busy. I sense that I may have a good measure of type A in my bones.

Type B's

Type B's are sometimes affectionately called "slugs." Their energy level may appear to be lower. Notice that I used the word "appear" in that sentence. Their energy is not necessarily less than a Type A; it is simply more focused. Type B's plan, anticipate and occasionally even procrastinate. Deciding not to decide is a decision. That is a perfectly appropriate way to deal with impending action. However, procrastination is different. Procrastination involves putting things off until they become a crisis. Type B's appear to have "less on their plate." Again, this is not necessarily true. Type B's can have many activities on their plate. Type A's are generally spinning many full plates at the same time. They are usually running from one place to another to make sure that the spinning plates do not fall crashing down onto the floor. Obviously, I am overstating both personality types by making a literary caricature of each. Type B's are not lazy, they just appear more "laid back."

I believe that I am more Type A in my personality type. Type B behavior can drive me crazy. For example, I hate fishing. Type B's seem to love "holding a rod waiting for a fish to show them a good time." I enjoy catching a fish. Who would not love ripping a hook out of a cold wiggling thing's mouth? I never understood how guys could go out in a boat with a few cases of beer and deep-sea fish. Yuck! Sitting in the sun chugging beers, bonding and yelling in unison, "It doesn't get any better than this!" is not my idea of a good time. Ice fishing really eludes my sense of good judgment. Who waits for a day cold enough to drive a truck on the ice to drill a hole and sit in sub-zero weather waiting for a tug on the line? And when the fisherman gets cold enough, he lights a fire on the ice. What am I missing here? In any case, my sons all seem to love fishing. They wanted to get up early one Saturday morning and go fishing on a local lake; the one morning I wanted to sleep in and they wanted to get up early enough to see the sun rise in the east. Well, we do things for our children. I set the alarm early, woke up cursing and enjoyed the chance to wake them out of a deep sleep to go fishing. "You wanna fish? Okay, then get up now!" They jumped out of bed as if they were lying awake waiting for me to awaken them. I was so disappointed. We arrived at the site just in time to see the sun beginning to rise. My classic type A behavior kicked in, as I rooted the sun on. I figured that I was stuck there all day until the sun sank into the western sky. As we sat there with red bobbers floating on top of the murky water, one of my sons said, "Hey Dad! Isn't this awesome?" I grunted back, "Oh yeah, this is a great time!" We sat there the entire day without one nibble. We did not catch a thing. We sat there baiting and re-baiting our hooks without the satisfaction of even a nibble. At last, the sun began to set. We had eaten much of our bait for lunch. It was now time to leave. I said, "Okay guys, let's clean up. It is time to go home!" Reluctantly my boys wearily collected their gear and headed to the car. We headed back home finally and I recall saying to myself, (thanking God to this day that I did not say this out loud) "What a wasted day this was! I didn't get one thing accomplished, I never even caught a fish!" I no sooner said that to myself, when I overheard Andy lean over Brian and say to Jeffrey, "Hey Jeffrey, wasn't this an awesome day! So fun fishing with Dad, huh?" I learned a tremendous lesson that day. Productivity is not always measured in terms of getting things done.

Sunbathing seems to be a popular recreational activity for Type B personalities. I never understood the notion of sunbathing as a way of relaxing. Imagine taking a blanket too disgusting to use in a bed and bringing it to a crowded beach. After trying to find a parking spot, paying $20.00 and then burning the white meat on the bottom of your feet as you scamper across the burning asphalt parking lot to get to the Sahara-like sand, you try to find the perfect spot under the sweltering heat of the sun. The first thing I do is sweat. I begin to perspire like a stuffed pig. Then, the wind begins to blow the sand and it sticks to my sweat. Then the horseflies find me and they start buzzing around my hot and sweaty body. Then, after you bake the front half of your body, you roll over and begin the process again on your backside. Yikes! I am getting nervous just writing this. If you are lucky, you get to spend the night spraying Solarcaine on your swollen red body suffering from the 1st degree burns that you just imposed on yourself from your day of relaxing in the sun. Once your sunburn heals, you get to peel skin and scratch an insatiable itch with any object such as a clothes hanger, long rulers, or anything else you can find to reach the middle of your back. To make this scenario even more appealing, we are now discovering how a lifetime of this can result in an often life threatening malignant melanoma. Now, this seems a high price to pay for sunbathing. When I go to the beach, or to a pool, I am constantly in the water. I figure if I go to the beach or pool, I am more interested in the water than I am in the sand or the concrete deck. Some Type B's I know could go to the beach and spend a year lying on the beach if the sun did not go from one end of the sky to the other.

My way of relaxing is flying a single engine airplane. On July 11, 1978, I received my private pilot's license. Few activities relax me more than flying through the sky at 5,000 feet at 110 knots viewing the earth from a perspective few people get to enjoy on a regular basis. I have flown lots of other people in my small aircraft who have not been nearly as relaxed as I am. This is my point. One's personality type would appear to dictate what kinds of activities relax us. While Type B's find sunbathing to be relaxing, I find it stressful. While I find flying a single engine aircraft to be relaxing, others find that stressful. I purchased a two seat Cessna 150 aircraft in 1980. I sold it and purchased a four seat Cessna 172 Skyhawk in 1997. Renting airplanes was not enough for me. I wanted to own an airplane so I could fly anywhere I wanted any time I wished without having to worry about returning the airplane so that somebody else could rent it. Admittedly, I have rarely flown my Cessna 172 Skyhawk with all four seats filled. Apparently there are not enough Type A personalities in my life to fill the seats in my airplane.

Just because we have certain personality types does not necessarily mean that our children will have the same personality. One of my sons is type A, one is type B and I have never figured out what Brian's personality could be called. Type A's call type B's, "slugs, couch potatoes, lazy, non-motivated, wimpy introverts." Type B's call Type A's, "Hyper, overactive, unfocused extroverts. Put them on medication." It always bothered me the way we treated overactive kids in our schools. It seemed to me that Ritalin was not the answer to the issue of little Type A's. I always had a tongue in cheek suggestion to the teachers who wanted to medicate their hyperactive kids. I suggested, "We should not drug the kids. Let's drug the teachers." Ironically, several teachers thought that was a great idea.

I believe that my divorce was, at least in part, a victim of my personality. I was driven to succeed. My need to become upwardly mobile and get ahead prompted my drive to continue my education and to work several jobs at the same time. I attended too many night meetings. I was driving into Boston at least twice a week to Boston State College to earn my Masters degree. I continued immediately after receiving my Masters by attending Northeastern University several days a week to pursue my Doctorate. Getting promoted from physical education teacher, 3rd grade teacher, teaching assistant principal, full-time assistant principal, principal and finally superintendent of schools simply reinforced my driven efforts. It was evident to everybody (except to me apparently) that my marriage was becoming a victim of my own ambition. In retrospect, I wish I had gone into marriage counseling with Judi. I give her credit in this regard. She suggested to me on at least several occasions that we go to counseling. Blinded by my own need to "succeed," I rejected her suggestion. Sadly, the day finally came to tell the boys that Mom and Dad were getting divorced. Under the Dunkin Donuts sign on Route 3A in Kingston, MA, I told my sons. Jeffrey cried uncontrollably, Andy wanted a chocolate doughnut and Brian just wanted to go home to ride his Big Wheel. It would appear that type A's and type B's often fall in love with each other, they marry and spend the rest of their lives driving each other nuts.

None of my adult sons are the least bit interested in flying or airplanes. When they were young, I used to fly them in the back of the plane rental and practice endless "touch and goes." These are simply practice drills for a new pilot to hone take off and landing skills. A touch and go is taking off, going around the airport traffic pattern (basically a series of rectangular turns called crosswind, downwind, base, and final), landing the airplane in the middle of the runway (hopefully), then taking off again before the airplane comes to a full stop. While the activity is exciting for new pilots, it is understandably boring to little boys. They typically slept in the plane as I took off and landed for what must have seemed like endless hours to them. When I purchased an airplane, you can only begin to imagine how difficult it was for me to get all three boys to hang out with me at the airport. As a result, I only had two rules for my sons when they came with me to the airport as I puttered around with my airplane: (1) My boys were not allowed to fight. Any parent with more than one child would understand the need for this basic ongoing rule, and (2), They were not to go near any spinning propellers. I figured I would keep the rules simple, few and easy to remember.

The boys made up a simple game. They would take turns seeing how long they could stay in the trunk of my car before getting frightened and having to get out. They were competing to see who could stay in the trunk the longest. This seemed like a benign activity to me, since after all, they would not be fighting and they would be safe from spinning propellers. I recall that the competition was particularly keen between Brian and Jeff.

Jeff closed the trunk on Brian as he curled up in the dark confines of the Ford Escort's small trunk area, sharing the space with a spare tire and assorted other pieces of accumulated junk. Jeff yelled out the time. "One minute," Jeff would announce. "Two minutes," Jeff barked out. Finally, a frantic knock on the inside of the trunk signaled Jeff to open the trunk door. Jeff announced that Brian remained in the trunk for 2 minutes and 35 seconds. The time was recorded on the dirty window with Jeff's finger. This was the standard that Jeff needed to beat. It was Jeff's turn to crawl into the trunk. Brian closed the trunk and began to keep track of the time. "One minute, two minutes, three minutes, new record, four minutes," and finally Jeff knocked on the inside of the trunk to get out. Brian announced that Jeff had the new record of 4 minutes and 15 seconds. The new record was duly recorded on the dirty window. Challenged, but inspired by Jeff's effort, Brian crawled back into the trunk, committed to setting a new record, but this time Jeff changed the rules. With Brian huddled in the trunk, Jeff tossed the keys into the trunk and then he shut the door. You can only imagine what happened next. Brian panicked. His bloody screams muffled from the closed trunk door caught my attention very quickly. Jeff was laughing as he tried to describe to me how he was "helping" Brian set a new record. For anybody who is familiar with older vintage Ford Escorts, you would know that the trunk and the back seat sections are separated by merely cardboard. I was able to easily free Brian from the trunk through the back seat of the car. Why did the game that was once fun turn into terror? What changed to make the notion of crawling into an automobile trunk so frightening? Obviously, it was the concept of control. The game was only fun when the option of "getting out" was in control of the person trapped in the darkness. Once that control was lost, the recreational nature of the game was lost. That is a very fine line between fun and terror. Horror movies can be fun because we can close our eyes. How much of our lives can we actually control? We cannot control the weather, being stuck in traffic, the economy, our bosses and, to some extent, the older our children get, the less control we have over them. This does not diminish our propensity to worry about our children, but it is a perspective that might help us better understand the chronic nature of parental stress.

Chapter 7: The Need For Closure

The brain is divided into two main hemispheres, a left and right cerebrum. The two major halves are connected underneath with a neuron sheath called the corpus callosum. The brain stem is below and behind the major brain hemispheres and includes, in part, the medulla, cerebellum and other components designed essentially for non-voluntary bodily functions. Without having to go into further details regarding issues such as specific motor control, short and long term memory, occipital lobes, limbic systems, parietal lobes and other anatomical parts that would require footnotes, let us go back to the left and right hemispheres. Perhaps it would be useful to differentiate, anecdotally, what would characterize left and right brain behavior.

Left brain people think differently than right brain people. They enjoy being organized, structured, and they love computers. They fantasize about being left alone with a good spreadsheet. They crave structure. They put money into their wallets in order, the 20's, the 10's, the 5's and the 1's. For some, that is not enough. All the presidents have to face the same direction. Left-brain people make up the "IT" people at work. Technology is their deity. Information, data, statistics and anything quantitative lures them into their dream world. Let us consider what this might look like. A left-brain person wakes up on a Saturday morning. Is it not amazing how easily we could sleep forever during the week, but the one morning we can sleep in, we wake up bug eyed? The grass could be growing up to our waist, the house could be filthy, but the quarterly report with the year-to-date expenditures is complete and ready for distribution. The left brainer jumps out of bed, startled with the thoughts of how many things need to be done. What is the first thing a left brainer does? Our left-brain friend makes a list. It is not enough just to make a list. The paper needs to be titled with bold lettering on the top of the page saying, "THINGS TO DO TODAY." Next, somebody in the house needs to see how many things are on the list and need to be done that day. "Look Honey, see how much I have to do today?" Proper protocol will result in a sympathetic, "You poor baby. How do you do it?" Left brainers are not done yet. Many put their list on a blackboard in the kitchen. While the family is sitting around the table eating breakfast, our left brainer is making his morning announcements.

Guess what list makers crave. They love checking things off. Some get rulers and red magic markers to draw straight lines through their accomplished list items. Others are satisfied with simple checkmarks. Some are so sick that they actually make little boxes just so they can check the middle of it. Some carry this to the extreme of actually putting things that they have already done at the top of their list, just to get the satisfaction of checking them off. Left brainers love closure. They love the satisfaction of getting things done. Making lists gives a visual reinforcement to things actually being accomplished. I suspect that in some cases the "crossing things off" becomes as satisfying as the actual act of "doing the task."

Right brainers tend to be tolerant of the ongoing nature of life. They are the artistic, sensitive and creative people in our lives. They tend to have wonderful imaginations. In the corporate world, the Human Resource Department may be more characterized with right brainers than left brainers. In our schools, left brainers tend to teach high school math, while right brainers tend to teach art in the elementary grades. I am speaking in absolutes here only to make my point. Obviously, all of us are, to varying degrees, combinations of traits depending on many factors including context, environment and perspective. Clearly, nobody is solely anything. This is perhaps what makes us so human. Nevertheless, consider the stress caused by a personality need to find closure in a job that offers little closure. For example, when is a salesperson ever really finished? When a successful sales associate reaches a specifically stated goal, how is he rewarded? Typically, he is faced with a higher more ambitious goal. Can you imagine a Vice President of Sales at any sales meeting taking the podium and making this announcement to the entire sales force? "I have an announcement to make regarding sales for the year. That's enough! We have plenty of revenue. Let us begin to level off in our sales efforts." When is a parent ever really finished parenting? At 18, they come back. At 21, they come back and they bring people with them! In any profession involving people and service, when is closure ever achieved? When is a teacher, social worker, nurse, doctor, truck driver, police officer or anybody ever really finished? Life is an ongoing process. We compartmentalize portions of our life to establish arbitrary time lines for closure. Whether it be a calendar year, a season, a quarterly report, an anniversary or a deadline, we are attempting to enjoy the sense of accomplishment associated with closure. Read any company mission statement and then ask, when is that vision truly accomplished with finality? Ever notice how much pleasure some people derive from making jigsaw puzzles? Think about what really happens. They go to Toys "R" Us and purchase a box with 87,000 assorted pieces. They bring the box home and spread all the pieces over the table, threatening everyone in the house to stay away from the puzzle. Then they spend the next two months of their lives sticking the pieces together. Usually, they like to start on the edges. Talk about somebody not getting out of the house enough! Think about what they end up with. Usually it is some beautiful landscape scene, a farmhouse, a moose or some other vision of interest. There is one interesting notion about this that I find curious. I would bet anything that the person putting the puzzle together knew exactly what the picture was going to look like before the puzzle was completed. After all, it was on the box when they bought it. The picture offers no surprise to the person investing all the hours putting the pieces together. Then why do some people enjoy jigsaw puzzles? I believe they enjoy finishing the puzzle. Again, the satisfaction of closure may be the primary motivation. If you want to frustrate the person putting the puzzle together, hide one piece right out of the middle. Maybe a jigsaw puzzle is a metaphor for life. We are all trying to make the many pieces fit, keeping the pieces together, and trying to find a sense of value by successfully finishing everything we start.

Chapter 8: What's With the Bag?

We have all heard of "Bag Ladies." I feel, however, that there are certain personalities in certain fields that actually could be called "Bag People." Typically, these folks work in jobs that have desks, involve a degree of ongoing tasks, and are usually overwhelmed by the many demands put upon them. Since my primary area of expertise is in public school education, I will use a classroom teacher as my example in this regard. Note, however, how readily the behavior can be applied generically to virtually any office, clerical or corporate setting.

The day is over. The buses have left and the classroom teacher is free to finally go home. On the desk are letters, notes, schedules, bus lists, special education forms, special consideration lists, memos, curriculum information, assessment surveys, worksheets, packets of school picture money, pink telephone message sheets, etc., etc.. Time to go home? Nope, not a chance. Good teachers cannot go home with all of those assorted items on their desk. They get a bag. Then, they scoop all the loose items and put them into the bag. Watch teachers leaving a school at the end of a day. You will see many of them lugging their bags to their cars. They bring their bag home every night, and they put the bag in the same spot in the house. This is the "bag spot." The bag remains untouched until it is lugged back to the school the next morning. The teacher then literally takes the items out of the bag and spreads them out all over the desk. You can also determine how long the teacher has been there by the quality of his or her bag. New teachers have canvas bags they picked up at a conference somewhere. They usually have a clever "If you can read this, thank a teacher" type statement embroidered on the bag. If the teacher has been around a while, he owns an L.L. Bean or Lands End bag. If the teacher is a veteran or an administrator, he carries a briefcase. These are simply bags with handles.

Why do we enjoy carrying things around with us? If we cannot finish things, then why not bring them home with us? It almost feels reassuring to know that the very source of our stress (the never ending paperwork) can be with us in the event we can ever get to it. Perhaps this gives us a measure of perceived control over the sources of our stress. Many of us worry about things over which we have absolutely no control. Why worry about the weather? Why worry about the economy? Why worry about other people and their problems? Would it not make more sense to worry about only those issues over which we had a measure of control? The ironic part about this is the fact that the more we care, the more we worry.

I recall driving on the Maine Turnpike to an evening speaking engagement. It was raining so hard, I could hardly see the lines on the road. There were a number of strategically placed safety signs on the center strips of the Maine Turnpike. I often wondered who writes these messages. Among them include the following helpful reminders: "Avoid sudden stops." Now that is a clever reminder. "Stay awake and alert." Hopefully you get to read this one before dozing off. "Rotate your tires." I assume the tires were rotating as you drove. "Dim your lights." In any case, the rain was so heavy, I had trouble reading the highway safety signs. I heard on the radio that there was a terrible multiple fatality automobile accident on Route 6 Eastbound near Exit 3. Oh my God! That is Brian's exit! Every parent knows what I did next. I called him on my cell phone for one very simple reason. I needed to hear his voice say, "Hello." I did. He did. Then I made up a lame excuse for checking in with him. The point here is quite simple. We never stop worrying about people we love. This form of stress is simply the price we pay for caring so much about others. The magazines say, "Don't worry about the stress." They suggest we should jog. Well, I will never jog. When I die, I want to be sick.

Chapter 9: If I am so happy, why am I crying?

It was November 1, 1998 when Karen and Brian invited me to go out to dinner. Now for everybody who has children, I have a suggestion. For all the aggravation they have provided for you, all the tuition they have cost you and all the sleepless nights you have had because of them, when they grow up and invite you to dinner, for goodness sake, go! That is the least they can do! We went down to Mashpee Commons. It is a nice retail shopping area off Route 6, Exit 3 off 151 before the New Seabury Circle. There are many very nice stores, specialty shops, and restaurants. There are two nice restaurants, "Gone Tomatoes" and "Bobby Byrnes." We typically ate at "Gone Tomatoes," not because of the food or the prices, but because we like the people. It is funny how that works. We tend to go back to places where the people are nice and where we feel comfortable. We had a nice dinner. Karen sat at the table and Brian sat across from her. I sat between the two of them. We talked, enjoyed the dinner, and I said to Brian, "Brian, are you glad that you bought a new house?" He said, "Dad, it is so exciting!" Brian and Karen had lived in an apartment and bounced back and forth between the apartment and my house. They met at college. After college, they dated and married. Yes, there is a God! I said, "Brian, when you bought the house, how did you feel?" He said, "Dad, it is wonderful! Owning your own home is so nice!" I said, "Well, good for you, Brian, but think of what you just did. You made a promise to a bank. For 30 years you are going to pay back a loan. Amortize the loan out over 30 years, and you will see that you will be paying for the house probably two or three times. Brian, try not paying your utilities on time; oil, gas, cable telephone. They will shut them off if you don't pay in a timely manner. And new construction does look nice, Brian, but let me tell you something, even new construction might settle, and when it does, you might have to pay unexpected maintenance bills. If you don't pay your mortgage on time, the bank will take your house away from you. Nice touch, huh?" Brian was not as happy about his new home. It is funny how that works. You can be excited about something and also stressed by the very same thing. I said, "Brian, let me put this meal on my American Express Card. It is my privilege to do so." Brian said, "Dad, put your credit card away. You will need to save your money." "Dad," he said, "It is my privilege to tell you that in July, you are going to be a Grampa." I could not believe it, a young hunk like me actually becoming a Grampa! I jumped to my feet and I started to cry. I never understood the notion of crying when you are happy. Miss America contests confuse me. The contestants spend all night trying to win, the winner gets crowned, and the first thing she does is she cries. The rest of them behind her lost and they are singing and dancing. It just does not make any sense to me. Now I understand. I was so happy, I was crying. Karen saw me crying. She jumped to her feet, she wrapped her arms around me, and we cried together. Brian saw us crying and he jumped to his feet. The three of us were standing at the table, crying and hugging, after dinner. Somebody must have thought we did not like the bill. It was wonderful. I was so happy. July 2nd was the due date. I was so excited! July 2nd, I am going to be a Grampa! Now, let me tell you something about being a single Dad of three sons. I missed a lot of little league games and school plays. As a school principal, I remember actually welcoming all the parents to the school plays and concerts, asking the parents, "Please sit back and enjoy the children. They are so talented and they are so excited that you are here this evening." Ironically my own son was crying in another schoolyard because I missed his solo clarinet performance. One spring, I actually taught parenting classes at the Governor John Carver School on Tuesday and Thursday nights, from 6:30 - 8:00 p.m., and I missed every single one of Andy's little league games teaching parents how to communicate with their children. So, I made a promise. When my grandchild is born, I will be home. I will be home in Lakeville, MA, not traveling and speaking elsewhere. I will be home for the birth of my grandchild. Here is what I did. Left-brain people will be very proud of me. I bought a Day Timer, a daily calendar and plan book, and I blocked off two weeks; the week before July 2nd and the week after July 2nd. That gives Karen two weeks to have the baby. I figured that ought to be enough. So, I started getting phone calls. "Mr. Bossio, will you come in and speak at 8:00...." and I interrupted them and said, "I'm sorry, I can't." "Mr. Bossio, would you be available to..." and I interrupted and said, "I'm sorry, I can't do that this year." Understand that I am self-employed. I am a sole proprietor. I get 1099's at the end of the year. I do not get a payroll check every Friday. I get paid only when I work. I pay my own life insurance and health insurance. I take vacations when I can. I have my own pension plan. Imagine somebody who is self-employed actually turning work away. That is exactly what I did. I promised I would be home for the birth of my grandchild. I am willing to give up work, even though I am the sole proprietor and owner of a small business. I was so excited about the big day!. July 1st came. The baby is going to be born the next day. I know, because after all it is in my Day Timer. The big day came, but obviously Karen did not see my Day Timer. She did not have the baby. I was so frustrated! It was as if somebody had cancelled Christmas on Christmas morning. July 3rd, no baby. July 4th, no baby. July 5th and still no baby! Then, I remembered, Brian never was good at math. He probably screwed up the calculations.   July 6th is my birthday. Would this not be cosmic? The baby will be born on my birthday.   We will bond instantly, sharing the same birthday for the rest of our lives.   Well, I had my birthday. Karen, as inconsiderate as she is, chose not to have the baby. The next day, July 7th, she had a doctor's appointment.   My office is the downstairs of my house.   Brian works full-time for me, and we sat in the office waiting for Karen to return from her doctor's appointment.   We looked at our watches and she was not here when she was supposed to be.   An hour later, she still had not arrived.   Two hours later, no call, no Karen, and we were both convinced that there must be a complication. Obviously, there must be something wrong!   It is interesting that if you are given enough free time to worry, you can actually begin to worry about problems that you do not have and problems you will never have.   A car pulled up.   It was Karen.   The door slammed.   Karen waddled into the office and she blurted out that the doctor indicated that she had not even begun to dilate yet!   Now, understand I have been dilating for a week and a half.   She said, "The baby hasn't dropped, the cervix has not softened, and she is not ready for the baby!" Now, I am not quite sure what this means, but as a man, this does not sound good. Then, I received a phone call from Danbury, CT, a federal penitentiary. "Mr. Bossio, a number of us have seen your videos and we have heard you speak. We would love to have you come to Danbury to speak to our inmate population of five- hundred inmates!" "But," he added quickly, "Don't worry." He said, "These are select inmates." Of course, I wondered to myself, "How select can they be?" Apparently these are the inmates who graduated from a drug rehab program, who will be pre-released into society over the next 12 months. "Mr. Bossio, would you come and speak to five-hundred inmates in Danbury, CT for three hours?" Now remember, I live in Lakeville, MA. That is at least a three-hour drive from Lakeville, MA to Danbury, CT to talk to five-hundred inmates for three hours and here is the killer! He admitted, "Unfortunately, Mr. Bossio, we have no money." Well, ordinarily each month I do two pro-bono speaking engagements for non-profit local human service agencies. But, this year I said, "I am unavailable. I cannot work. I'm sorry!" "Mr. Bossio, Please," he said, "No one speaks to inmates." I pondered and said, "Of course, I certainly understand that!" So, what am I going to do?

Chapter 10: Am I a Slushball?

Have you ever done anything at work that needed to be done but was not on your job description? Have you ever done anything that was not on your job description, but clearly on somebody else's? You know, however, that they would make life miserable for both of you if you asked, so you simply did it yourself. Have you ever volunteered to do something for which you neither have the time nor the interest, but it benefited someone else? If you said yes to these three questions, you may be a "slushball." A slushball is somebody who would rather inconvenience himself as opposed to bothering somebody else. Slushballs have real trouble saying no. I am afraid that I might fall into this category.

I suspect that slushballs know exactly what my response was to the Danbury Federal Penitentiary request to see if I would drive over three hours to speak to 500 inmates for three hours without receiving any honorarium for my service. Of course, I said, "Yes, I will." The moment the words came out of my mouth, I regretted them. I wanted to somehow put the words back. I said a big time curse! Obviously the second grader mentioned earlier and I became cosmically linked. The day came quickly. It was July 14th. For those of you from French heritage, ask your families what happened to the necks of your relatives on that day. July 14th is Bastille Day.

July 14th arrived and I dreaded the day. I was not looking forward to this day. Remember, I am the one who agreed to do this! The last thing in the world I wanted to do on this day was to drive six hours round trip to speak to 500 incarcerated inmates for three hours and receive absolutely no remuneration for doing so! Nevertheless, the day arrived. Ever notice how quickly days we dread arrive? Why would I agree to do this?

I agreed to do this, so here we go! I headed North on Route 24 to Route 495 North. I ventured North on Route 495 to Exit 22, Massachusetts Turnpike. Next, I drove west on Route 90, Mass Pike, to Exit 9 (Sturbridge, Route 84 West for the rest of my life). I headed West on Route 84 to Sturbridge over the Massachusetts/Connecticut line through Union, Stafford Springs, Vernon, East Hartford, Hartford, West Hartford, Farmington, New Britain, Waterbury, Newtown and finally, Exit 6, Danbury, CT. I journeyed about ½ mile to Route 37 and turned left onto Route 37 for about two miles to a hairpin turn at the Citgo Station. I turned right at the hairpin turn for about 3 miles until I saw a reservoir on the left at 9 o'clock, Dunkin

Donuts in a plaza at noon, and high up on the hill, at 3 o'clock, was the prison. If you know Connecticut, you know that I am not making this up. Those directions are 100% accurate.

There it was. It did not look like a corporate office. It was a prison; dark, steel, stone, barbed wire and guns. There was a big sign that said, "Welcome." I noticed a 7-inch wide cement walkway surrounded by beautifully landscaped grass and a sign that only the Federal Government could write, "Warning! Federal Property. Do not walk on grass. Remain on walkway. Penalty $10,000.00, 5 years imprisonment or both." Obviously, I planned on staying on the walkway. It is one thing to do this for nothing. It is another thing to spend 5 years in prison and pay $10,000.00 for doing so! Of course, being the Type A personality that I am, I sneaked a quick touch of the grass and headed up the cement walkway.

As I walked up the walkway, I noticed security cameras on either side tracking me. Apparently my motion activated an electrical circuit driving a small motor called a servo. A security camera attached to the servo tracked me as I moved. It takes little to amuse me. I stopped walking to see if the camera stopped. I walked backwards to see how responsive the cameras were. I even tried faking left and right like a basketball player to see the responsiveness of the electrical circuits. At one point, I actually jumped in front of the camera, stuck out my tongue, and thumbed my nose. After all, who cares? Nobody was looking!

Finally I reached the front door. While public buildings typically have glass foyers designed by architects to make people feel welcome, a prison simply has a steel door. It slid open electronically as I approached. I was not greeted with a customer service representative saying, "May I help you?" I was greeted by a guard who simply said, "You must be Bossio! We have all been watching you on closed circuit TV." Then, they assigned me the most massive armed guard I have ever seen.

This guard was massive. The guard had to be 6' 8" inches tall and weighed around 450 lbs. I have never seen such a classic mesomorph. The guard had a jutting chin, a huge bulging forehead, massive shoulders and no neck. This body skipped the neck and went directly into a head. This head appeared to be the shape of a perfect square. The sides went straight up from the shoulders, then turned 90 degrees to form the top of the head. A flat top haircut emphasized the square shape. On top, teetered a guard hat. Massive biceps were so large that the uniform was ripping apart at the seam. Triceps were bulging out under the arm with all three ligaments so well developed, you could see them clearly attached to the olecranon process. The guard had a 28" waist framed with a perfect "6-pack" rectus abdominus, rippling oblique muscles and latissimus dorsi running right up the back. The guard's butt was a perfectly formed gluteus maximus (and it was a maximus). The upper thighs had perfect quads with rippling hamstrings behind and a well-formed gastrocnemius bulging over the tall black boots. The guard wore a thick black belt with a walkie-talkie, keys, chains, nightsticks, and guns strapped down to the inner thighs. I am telling you. She was massive! I was then escorted to the gymnasium. I love gymnasiums. They are typically clean and bright. But, this gym was different. It was dirty and smelled of urine and foul body odor. The lighting was dark and oppressive. The inmates were all sitting quietly looking forward, dressed in brown nondescript outfits with numbers embroidered over the left front shirt pocket. The worst thing I saw, however, was 500 inmates and not one of them was looking at me! I was appalled! I drove all the way from Lakeville, MA to Danbury, CT to speak for three hours for no fee, and they were not going to even look at me? I do not think so! I jumped out from behind the podium and moved out to the floor so I could move throughout the inmates. I never like to use podiums. They make me look short and bald.

Chapter 11: What am I doing here?

Not looking at someone is the height of indifference. Would you buy anything from anybody if they did not look directly into your eyes? If you look at someone's face, you will see his heart. If you look into his eyes, you will see his soul. I have driven too far to speak too long to too many people for too little financial gain to be treated this way. Inmates or not, I wanted them to at least look at me. That was basic courtesy and I figured I deserved at least that.

I walked out among the inmates. I gently teased several of the inmates in my efforts to engage their attention. They loved it! The energy in the room increased. More and more of the inmates were interested in who was going to be teased next. It was working. I was getting their attention. Then, I broke all prison rules. I actually touched an inmate. I patted one inmate's back in an encouraging and sympathetic way. Visitors are never allowed to come into physical contact with an inmate at any time. However, no guard stopped me. Now, every inmate was looking at me. It was obvious that they were enjoying my efforts to gain their attention. They came alive with excitement. They laughed at the right times. They were generous in their responses to my theatrics. One of the best things about public speaking is the fact that the speaker always knows how the speech is going. Only the speaker can see every face in the room. Faces say everything. You cannot hide passion. You also cannot hide indifference. Our faces say more than medical records, permanent record folders, bank accounts, credit reports, criminal records or academic transcripts. At the very least, we can look at people when they are talking to us (and when we are talking to them). A smile on our face can only be a bonus. It was obvious that my speech was going extremely well. The inmates were loving every minute of it. I was energized. I feed off the energy of my audiences. I have a feeling we go through our lives feeding off the energy of others, or the lack of other people's energy. Maybe this explains why miserable people tend to hang out with other miserable people.

The three hours flew by. I received a thunderous standing ovation from the inmates. It felt so wonderful to witness a transition from total indifference to generous appreciation. I was enthralled. As the inmates filed out of the gymnasium, they formed a line to thank me. One inmate said to me, "Thank you man! I haven't laughed in two years!" One inmate whispered to me, "I haven't smiled in months!" Then, something remarkable happened. An inmate broke one of the prison's most enforced rules. The inmate touched me with a grateful pat to my back saying, "Norm, are you coming back sometime?" Inmates are never allowed to come into physical contact with a visitor. Again, however, no guard seemed to notice. I have since received many letters from the inmates. One letter talked about a son graduating from high school and the inmate had not seen him since he was in the sixth grade. One letter talked about a parent who died without saying goodbye. These letters do not get thrown away.

It is now time to leave the prison. I felt wonderful. Have you ever had a day when you felt that you really helped another person? Ever feel like you touched someone else's life? This was my day. I am going to ask you three questions. These are not rhetorical questions. Please answer them to yourself. When I walked into the prison, was I feeling stressed? When I walked out of the prison, was I feeling wonderful? How much money did I receive? Yes, I felt stressed entering Danbury Federal Prison. Yes, I felt wonderful leaving the prison, and they did not pay me a penny for my work! Money is not a motivator. We are truly motivated by doing good for others and feeling grateful appreciation for our efforts.

I floated on "cloud nine" to my car. I smiled to myself as the sun glowed off the top of my balding head. It does not get any better than this. Then it ended. The moment I spotted my car, it all changed. I whined to myself, "I have a three hour drive ahead of me!" I uttered the dreaded "F" word. I turned miserable immediately. What I am about to state here is 100% true, as an Appeals Court in Southern California ruled, I cannot utter out loud in the public sector, "So help me God!" I unlocked and opened my car door. I slammed the door behind me. I shoved the keys into the ignition and vigorously turned the key to start the car. I complained out loud, "What am I doing here? Why the hell did I drive all this way to speak to all of these inmates for nothing?" Immediately, my car phone rang. I picked up the phone and it was Brian. "Dad, 8 lbs, 6 oz. Colin Christopher Bossio has just arrived!" Yes, I am a Grampa.

On July 14, 1999, this is what I learned. When we take whatever gift we have and we use it to help people we do not even know, when we are inconvenienced to help strangers, when we say yes to help underdogs, and when we are motivated to do good......we WILL be paid. I do not know when, how or who actually decides, but I am convinced that we all get paid when we do good. I was paid handsomely for that day I spent in Danbury, CT. I know the directions now to Danbury, CT because I returned to do additional work. I was reminded when leaving to fill out tax forms. Since I am a contract service, I am a vendor to the prison and I would need to have my social security number and address on file, so I could receive a 1099 at the end of the year. The law requires this documentation for income exceeding $600.00. Somehow, I could not get myself to fill out the form. After all, I was already paid for my work that day. I now believe in a cosmic payroll.

Chapter 12: 9/11

I have very little patience for self-serving miserable people. I will now tell you why. On Wednesday, September 11, 2001, I flew out of Boston Logan Airport that morning. I flew out of Boston Logan Airport on an early morning Delta flight. I departed Boston at around 8:00 a.m., only minutes before American Flight 11 taxied down the same taxiway. I spent five days in Atlanta, GA and I almost caught myself complaining until I turned on the hotel television and saw what happened to over 3,000 Americans in a field in Western Pennsylvania, in an odd shaped building in Washington, DC, and in two towers in downtown Manhattan. I stopped complaining immediately. Delta Airline gave us overnight bags with shaving cream, toothpaste, and assorted other items in clear tubes. Of course, the first morning I brushed my teeth with the shaving cream! I thought it tasted sort of strange, but it seemed to clean up my teeth very well. It was now time to go home. I could not go back to Boston Logan Airport because the airport was still closed. I was scheduled to return back to Providence Airport. That is Green Airport, Exit 13 on Route 95 South of Providence, RI. I was picked up by Brian. Brian picked me up in his 1990 vintage Toyota Tercel. It was red with faded paint, a dent in the back, egg sandwich under the front seat, and five soiled pampers rotting under the towels in the back. Two more payments, and that bad boy was going to be his. But this time, I did not really complain about the soiled pampers. I wrapped my arms around my son and we simply hugged. We did not care who looked. Brian drove me back to Boston Logan Airport to pick up my car. Unfortunately, security took my car. It was not there. I parked in terminal B. For anybody who is familiar with Boston Logan Airport, that is the terminal for American Airlines. The man who parked to the right space beside me and the woman who parked on the left side of me at 8:44 a.m. on American Flight 11 hit tower #1. I was a parking spot away. Can you imagine if Social Security Administration in Lexington, Kentucky, Office for Hearings and Appeals put me on American or United? Who would be around to make sure that the grandchildren were taken care of? We are a parking spot away from tragedy. Again, life does not change by those things we worry about. It changes with life surprises. A telephone call in the middle of the night from an emergency room of a hospital can change your life forever.

So, I was off to get my car. Security had actually towed it. They towed it to Suffolk Downs, a local dog track, very close to the airport. We went to get my car. I was a mess! My suit was wrinkled, my shirt was wrinkled, my tie was off, and what little hair I have was sticking straight out the side! Ever have one of those days where you really do not want anyone to see you? Well, frankly, that was my day! And who greeted us? Fox Cable News Network TV crew. They came running over to see me. In this condition, I really did not want anyone to see me. They came running over, put on the camera, stuck the microphone up to my mouth and asked me what happened. I was absolutely appalled and embarrassed. So, of course, I picked up the microphone and gave them a 35-minute "freebie." I talked about Jeffrey, Brian and Andrew. I talked about Colin and yes, one more (Brian and Karen did it again!). I added a little girl, Makayla Ashley Bossio. Colin has a younger sister. She was born August 27th. I guess it sometimes takes tragedies to remind us what things are really important to us. There were a lot of phone calls made that day from the World Trade Center. I bet not one of them talked about the Dow Jones or the condition of mutual funds. I bet I am not the only person that day who talked about those things that really matter.

Chapter 13: "I Know"

Colin and Makayla surely changed this Grampa. Typically, on Saturday nights, I now babysit. I do not do so because it is on a Grampa's job description, I was never asked! I just simply chose to do so. In the interest of total disclosure, there are two reasons why I chose to babysit. First of all, and most apparent, is the fact that I want to spend time with my grandchildren. The second reason, however, is more subtle. I want Brian and Karen's marriage to last forever. I figure if I can give them one night a week to be lovers and friends, then I have done my part to help. Tucking the kids in at night has evolved into a clear protocol. Makayla must be covered in her princess covers, reminded not to let the "bed bugs bite," and assured and reassured that Grampa will leave the door open wide enough to let the hall light shine in on her face. Colin, however, requires more specific actions. Colin's transition from the crib to the "big boy" bed was not an easy one. He always seemed to prefer the self-contained crib to the "expanse" of the "big boy" bed. Waking up dry five days in a row was not enough ambitious a criteria, since even Grampa would be happy with that accomplishment! Colin's head must be down towards the south end of the crib, since the security monitor was placed on the north end of the crib. Colin had to face the window heading towards Margaret's house, his next-door older playmate. Apparently Colin already likes older women! Grampa bought the monitor when Colin was born so he could watch him sleep. It is amazing how much we worry about those we love. I recall buying Brian's first baseball cup when he was a catcher in little league. I worried about him getting hurt from a foul ball or a thrown bat. Brian was so proud of his new cup. He actually wore it on the outside for the first game! He even let his teammates hit him on his new cup to prove that it didn't hurt. I also recall buying Brian's first bulletproof vest when he became an auxiliary police officer. Again, the price we pay for loving people is the fact that we will worry about them forever. Now, it is time for Colin to go to bed.

After his piggyback ride upstairs, his careful placement in bed (similar to how a pizza is carefully placed into an oven), and a handy cup of water, Grampa is now tasked with the challenge of covering Colin with his blankets. The first blanket is the blue blanket with the buggies on it, placed under his chin and extended to cover his feet. The second blanket is the pink one with the white stripes, more casually placed from the waist down. The ratty white one can be placed anywhere, but typically its role is to cover the feet. Tiger needs to be placed on Colin's head in a position that allows the tail to hang towards Colin's right side.   In this way, Colin can take his pronated right hand, supinate his palm, grab the tail, and rub his cheek until he falls asleep.   Now that Colin is asleep, it is time to hit the light.   However, as I reach to hit the switch, a little voice says, "Grampa, Mommy lies next to me!"   Now, what am I supposed to do?   So, I lie next to Colin on the floor wondering how long I will have to be doing this.   As I lie there, I wonder when I can leave.   As we lie there together, Colin tells me long stories without endings.   They go on and on and on.   I wonder to myself, "Why do children tell us long stories without endings?"   I can only come up with two answers. Children tell us long stories without endings so that we will stay there and we will listen to them.

My mother, suffering from advanced stages of Parkinson's disease, is unable to drive, has difficulty walking, and prefers to stay home.   She is a stubborn blue-eyed Irish Mom who is fiercely independent.   When I take her to lunch, she does something that has become an ironic curiosity for me.   She sits there and tells me long stories without endings.   It occurs to me that she does so for the same reason as Colin.   She wants me, her only child, to stay and listen.   Apparently we never outgrow the need for people we care about to stay and listen to us.   My guess is that many people may or may not care about our ability to fix their problems, but they do hope that we stay and listen to them. My sense is that for many people, that is enough.

Colin's silence and heavy breathing prompts my exit from his bedroom. As I slowly and carefully get up to hit the lights, a little voice says, "Mommy rubs my neck!" As he lies in his crib and I am gently rubbing his neck, Colin repeats many of his never ending stories, but this time he has added a few never ending songs. This time, I changed my strategy. I decided to wait him out. I am going to stay there until he finally falls asleep. After what seemed like forever, Colin stopped talking and singing. His little expressive face became angelic. His breathing became slow and heavy. He turned his head to the left, leaving his right cheek pressed to the sheets. Obviously, he has fallen asleep. Time for me to hit the lights? No. Not all human behavior is rational. In fact, I believe it is one of the things that makes us so human. I did not get up to hit the lights. Imagine this. I wait all this time for Colin to fall asleep so I can hit the lights and leave. But instead, he falls asleep and I decide to stay and talk to him. Now, how dumb is that? I wait for him to fall asleep to talk to him, and I talk to him in a voice that is so quiet, I do not want to risk waking him up. I said to Colin, "Grampa loves you!" But, he was not sleeping.

He said something that I will never forget. The moment I finished telling Colin that I loved him, he opened his eyes, turned his head, looked up at me and said, "I know." Is that not enough? Maybe it is not important that people tell us that they love us back. Maybe it is more important that they know how much they are loved.

Chapter 14: Being Regular is not Enough

Every once in a while a speaking engagement is booked someplace that is really fun. Speaking in Cancun, Puerto Vallarta, Honolulu, Las Vegas and Los Cabos, Mexico are just several examples of the many memorable places where I have spoken. Clearly, they are more fun than speaking at a local Lions Club. The call I received from a professional banking association was potentially one of these jobs. Speaking in Florida, all expenses paid, a 5-digit honorarium, to hundreds of bankers throughout the country would be more exciting than speaking to 35 Lions Club members after they had dinner, five beers and just realized that all, but one of them, lost the door prize raffle for a $25.00 gift certificate to a local bait shop.

The problem with the speaking engagement in Florida, however, was the fact that the job was scheduled for the day after Halloween. A little boy named Colin had already beaten the bankers to Grampa. Colin had already called and asked me to trick or treat with him on Halloween night. Obviously, I would be unable to catch a flight in time to be ready to speak the next morning at the bankers conference. According to child pedagogy, long term memory goes back to about 4 years old. This means that 4-year-old Colin will remember what Grampa does from this point on. I also learned that the government cannot print enough money to break the heart of a child who adores you. However, I do not want to be a regular Grampa. I do not want to be a regular public speaker. Frankly, I do not want to be a regular anything. Comic books and movies are never made about a caped superhero with a big "R" on his chest. Corporate mission and vision statements would never have the word "regular" in them. I was not a regular teacher, principal or daddy. I was not going to start being regular as a Grampa. I decided to dress up with the kids for Halloween.

I drove to a local party and costume store. After a few minutes looking through the wide variety of costume options, I found the perfect one. This Grampa was going to be Spider Man. I paid $149.00 for this professional costume. At that price, I assumed that the costume would be a high quality loose fitting cotton deal. I could not have been more wrong! When the back of this costume was zipped at the back, there were no surprises under there! The bright red and blue costume clung to my body like a coat of latex paint! If a dime were placed between my thigh and the costume, it would be easy to read the date on the coin!

Finally, Halloween night had arrived. I drove to my mother's house since I promised to let her be part of the holiday festivities. She seemed rather amused, if not pleased, to see her adult only child bulging through the Spider Man costume. I wanted to dress my mother up as a witch. I have always had that fantasy. We drove down the Cape for the big night. When Spider Man and his mother pulled up in a cranberry colored Nissan Maxima, the kids went crazy. As we journeyed through the neighborhood, I noticed how many people were surrounding Spider Man and pointing at him. Even adults were aiming their flashlights at me. I am sure that they were laughing with me. Brian was making sport of me, saying that I was registered with the local police department and that I was doing well in my rehab program. As the adults opened their doors to give us the candy treats, I heard shrieks of amusement. Well, I hope they were amused and not horrified! Since Brian was with us every step of the way, I told him, "Go home and help Karen give out the candy at your house!" I assured him I would stay with the kids. At that point, Brian stopped in his tracks, pointed at my crotch and said, "Dad, this is my neighborhood. I do not want my neighbors to think that's me under there!"

Driving from Lakeville to Braintree, to West Barnstable, back to Braintree and finally home to Lakeville was not very convenient. Over 200 miles driving on Halloween night was not particularly fun; however, it made my mother very happy, pleased Colin and Makayla, and entertained the entire neighborhood. The Halloween tradition has since been followed by my annual visits as Batman and Darth Vader. Mom has been too tired to make the Halloween trips again. It is funny how many times that life's most inconvenient challenges become the most important things that we do.

Consistent with my need to not be a regular anything and to make my schools fun and wondrous places for both children and adults, I came up with an idea to make the Christmas season more festive for everybody. I wish I could come up with a better reason for this idea, but I cannot think of one. I have tried to rationalize this by thinking of a curriculum integration model. But, if I were totally honest with myself, I would have to admit that such an academic justification would be a stretch, at best. I wanted to fly into the playground in a helicopter dressed as Santa Claus on the last day of school before the winter recess vacation. Of course, I had neither a Santa costume, nor a helicopter. But, the idea sounded like fun, especially for me. I also wanted to do this as a surprise to the children and school staff. Now, I had to find a helicopter. Surprisingly enough, this was easy. Since the school was near a major automobile dealership and it was well known that they had a corporate helicopter, I would simply drive over, introduce myself, pray to God, gulp, and just ask. I did and to my surprise, they said yes to my request. I am not sure what would be worse, the disappointment of them saying no, or the terror of them saying yes. Motivated by the ease in which I secured a helicopter, I also found a Santa outfit to borrow for the big day. So, here was the plan. Only my secretary, the auto dealership, and a neighbor who lives next door to the school would know the details of the plan. I needed a place to change into the Santa Claus suit, and the neighbor next to the school was also on the School Committee and an active parent volunteer. She would be a perfect comrade for the surprise Santa visit. The school secretary was going to sound the fire drill alarm (She was to notify the fire department that it was merely a drill.). Prior to the alarm, she was to instruct the teachers over the loudspeaker system to make certain that everyone wore their coats, exited the building in an orderly fashion, and made a huge circle around the perimeter of the school baseball field. The police were also notified that a helicopter would be landing on town property. I was so excited when the helicopter left the parking lot of the Rodman

Ford Dealership. I could feel my heart pounding under all the pillows. As we approached the school field, I began to notice the ring of children. They looked like a wreath of gorgeous color. My eyes welled up. It was, for some reason, very emotional for me. The pilot circled the field lower and lower. The children began to notice Santa's bright red outfit and they began to literally jump up and down in unbridled glee. I was told later that many of the teachers were moved emotionally by the scene of Santa making a surprise visit to the school and the extraordinary reaction of the children. Santa was greeted by the school superintendent and a student from the special needs resource room. Santa was then escorted into the school media center and he met with all the children in the kindergarten through grade two classes. I figured children any older would recognize that "Mr. Bossio voice." Among my many wonderful memories of being a school principal, my helicopter Santa Claus visits rank very high. In every school where I served as principal, Santa made his holiday visit. I even asked the famed legal defense attorney, F. Lee Bailey if I could borrow his helicopter for this purpose. Although quite gruff in his manner, he generously provided a helicopter and a pilot for this purpose. Not all of Santa's visits were, however, without controversy.

In one of the three schools where I served as principal, a 5th grade male teacher made an appointment to discuss with me Santa's impending helicopter visit. This teacher was one of the most experienced, popular and effective teachers on my staff. He was passionate about teaching and everybody (including me) valued his opinions and input on all matters related to the school. My relationship to him was one of mutual respect. As a result of this context, you can only begin to imagine how surprised I was to hear his opinion on my Santa Claus helicopter visit. He was dead set against my doing this. Since he was Jewish, he felt that introducing Santa to the school culture was inappropriate, since this reinforced the Christian emphasis of the season in a school which is public and, as such, should only recognize the season in a secular manner. He said that he was personally offended and he hoped I would cancel the event. I took his comments personally. He was very respectful and professional in his manner and tone. In fact, part of me wished he had been irrational, disrespectful, and unreasonably confrontational. This was the first and only negative feedback I had ever received regarding the annual tradition. I was crushed. I certainly understood and respected his perspective. He was questioning the entire propriety of having such a non-secular symbol in a secular setting. While I disagreed with his premise, I certainly understood why he would feel this way. He gave me a lot to think about. Part of me wanted to rationalize that he was only one person, and the only person who ever criticized this event, at least openly. On the other hand, history has proven that one person can change the world. I had a dilemma. I did not want Santa's visit to polarize my staff and community, and I would never want to alienate a child for any reason. He followed up our conference with a well written letter summarizing and documenting his feelings. There is nothing worse than receiving a beautifully written letter with narrative that almost poetically stated an adversarial philosophical view. I seriously considered canceling the event.

Several days later, a 5th grade student wanted to meet with me. He was a bright articulate young man, whose teacher had met me earlier regarding Santa's visit. Also Jewish, the youngster told me how uncomfortable the Santa visit was making him. How do you debate a sincere 5th grade student? I told him that I viewed Santa as a more cultural symbol of the holidays, rather than a religious symbol of the Christian celebration of Jesus' birth. He retorted by reminding me that Santa Claus would not be coming down his chimney this year. He did say, however, that there will be a Menorah on his fireplace. Yikes! Life was so much simpler when I was a gym teacher. Let's see, should we play "Duck, Duck, Goose" today or "Red Rover, Red Rover?" I thanked him for meeting with me and letting me know how he felt. Like his teacher, he followed up with a beautifully crafted letter. His Mother also wrote me a letter stating her displeasure with my plans for Santa's visit to the school. I did not sleep well for several nights. It is hard to dispel sincere adversarial opinions. After a week of great personal ambivalence, I made the decision.

I decided to meet the teacher and inform him of my decision. I also met with the youngster and told him what I had decided. I followed up both meetings with a letter outlining my decision making process. I also responded to the Mom's letter citing, describing, and explaining my difficult decision to go through with Santa's helicopter visit to the school. I decided that while I certainly understand, respect, and accept the feelings of those who do not celebrate the birth of Jesus, I did believe that Santa Claus had emerged into a more social icon and as such, was not being forced upon anybody within an exclusive religious context of Christian theology. It was supposed to be fun! There were no hidden insidious theological messages. The variant points of view of my Jewish colleagues did, however, provide for me a conscience and required me to further contemplate the enormous responsibilities of those of us who engineer public policy, particularly in a society so rich in diverse points of view. I recall a number of important lessons that this principal learned.

1.   Every decision maker needs to have a conscience.

2.   It is much easier to be regular. It takes a measure of risk to be special.

3.   Not everyone is going to agree with even the most well meaning courses of action.

4.   It is important that we listen and consider the opinions of everybody.

5.   Sometimes the majority can be wrong. It is possible that the quiet voice of a child carries more wisdom than the empowered.

6.   It is important to think carefully about whose needs are being met through public policy. Was I flying into the schools as Santa because it was fun for me, or was I doing it for the children?

7.   Schools need to be fun for everyone.

8.   I refuse to go through my life as a regular anything.

Chapter 15: The Ring Bearer

My youngest son, Andrew, had been dating Vikki since the 9th grade. Frankly, that is either really romantic or sick. Painfully shy, young Andy met a blonde junior high classmate who was equally as shy as he was. I recall Vikki driving by my house to see Andy, but she was too shy to do anything but park her car on the street in front of my house and wait for Andy to notice her. Once I remember going outside to introduce myself to Vikki. When she noticed me approaching her car, she sped off. Let me be clear here, however, to assure everybody that Vikki has certainly outgrown her shyness, at least with me. Clearly, this was a match made in heaven. I am convinced that they are perfect for each other. As a result, I was not surprised when they became engaged to be married. The big day was September 21st. The wedding was going to be at Our Lady of the Lakes Church in Halifax, MA, with the reception being held at the Pembroke Country Club. The ring bearer was, of course, going to be Colin. Since Andy is Colin's Godfather, Colin seemed a natural choice to serve this role at Andy's wedding. Three-year-old Colin was going to be the perfect choice. The first challenge was to purchase Colin's tuxedo. I drove to South Shore Plaza in Braintree to find the perfect tuxedo. The problem with tuxedos for children this young is the fact that you have to buy them. There are no tuxedos available to rent that would fit 3-year-old children. So, I bought Colin's tuxedo. Three-T (toddler size) seemed to be the perfect fit. He was going to look so adorable in his black jacket with silk trim, baggy black trousers with an elegant stripe running down his leg, a fluffy white shirt with a black bow tie, and a snazzy white carnation on his left lapel.

It had rained the night before the wedding; however, the skies cleared up beautifully as we all arrived at the church in the morning. As I stepped out of the car, Colin noticed me and started running the full length of the massive hardtop parking lot outside the church. I winced as he splashed through what seemed like every puddle of water in the lot. I could tell from Karen's face that she was not pleased. I could only imagine how much time she spent getting Colin and little Makayla dressed and ready for the wedding.

Guys were doing what guys do at functions like these. Have you ever noticed how many men always seem to clump with men during events like this? Guys seem to enjoy standing, chatting, sitting and basically just hanging out together. I am not sure if it is the "male bonding" thing going on or if nobody else wants to be seen with them. In any case, the "guy clumps" were beginning to form at Andy and Vikki's wedding. One notable clump was at the huge front door of the church. I was part of this clump. There were about ten of us standing around solving the world's problems and giving advice on such world matters as the Red Sox, Patriots, Celtics and Bruins, and the outrageous escalation of gas prices. Of course, we were all dressed in our rented tuxedos, due back on Monday by 6:00 p.m. or else the tuxedo rental store would begin encumbering our children. There were days in my life when that notion would have sounded pretty good to me. But I digress.

All of a sudden, one of the men in the clump asked me if I thought that Colin would really walk down the aisle by himself holding the rings. I said, "Of course. Absolutely! Colin knows what to do and he will do it without any assistance!" I may have sounded a bit defensive, but after all, I am the Grampa. The challenger retorted that Colin is much too young to understand his role. I raised my voice, postured myself and exclaimed, "Colin is a smart little boy and he understands his role in the wedding!" Our voices became louder. We escalated our energy level and we did something I am not very proud of. We made bets. We took book on whether Colin would walk down the aisle without assistance. I figured, why not make this wedding interesting? Ten-dollars apiece would make this wedding more interesting to any guy wanting a piece of the action. We all kicked in 10-dollars. One fellow served as a treasurer. He stuffed his pockets with all of the cash. Now, we have a problem. With money involved, we need to document our bets on paper. However, we had no paper to formalize the betting action.

So, somebody (not I) ran into the church and "borrowed" a hymnal. Remember, I did not do this, someone else did. The blank back page was ripped out of the book. I know that this sounds sacrilegious (and perhaps it may be), but at least now we have our paper to record our bets. Our bets were now recorded. Most of the betters put their money on Colin not walking down the aisle without an adult to accompany him.

It was now time for the formality of the wedding. The wedding party formed a straight line in the back of the church. We were instructed to walk into the church when the organ music started and to remain standing until the organ stopped. It would then be time for the bride to walk down the aisle. We practiced this the night before at the wedding rehearsal dinner. I remember all the details, since I paid for the dinner, open bar, and all. The music started. I was so proud. This was my third son's wedding. They were all educated, they all had jobs and now they would all be married. Yes, there is a God! I knew exactly where to stand. The music stopped. Now it was Vikki's turn.

Vikki looked absolutely gorgeous. She was dressed in the most beautiful white gown. She looked so different! There were no ripped sweat pants, no sneakers with blue paint and no baggy sweatshirt. Her face was elegantly covered with a white veil. Her Daddy was at her side to give her away. It was a magical moment. Of course, I just wanted to get her the hell out of the way, so we could get to the real action!

Now, it was Colin's turn. He stood there at the end of the aisle holding the pillow and the rings. I gulped in horror. He was not moving. He seemed frozen in terror. I felt like Grampa at a dog track. I felt like waving my arms and yelling, "Come on, big guy! One time for Grampa!" Suddenly, out of nowhere, Karen appeared. Yes, Colin's Mom, Karen, knew exactly what to do. She whispered something in Colin's ear. Immediately he briskly walked down the aisle without the slightest hesitation up to the altar. I found out later what Karen had done. She put a candy bar in Colin's pocket and told him, "Go up to Daddy and he will open it for you." Daddy (Brian) was Andy's best man. Can you believe it? I won $190.00. Karen is a genius. She knew exactly how to motivate Colin. He did not walk down the aisle because it was on his job description. He walked down the aisle because there was a candy bar for him. Maybe we need to begin to understand what are our "candy bars." My guess is that successful salespeople spend a lot of time trying to figure out what their customers' "candy bars" are. It is such an elegantly simple lesson in human motivation and behavior. It is amazing to think that it took a little preschooler to teach me.

Chapter 16: The Wedding Blessings

Families are systems of ongoing traditions and rituals. The Bossio's are no exception in this regard. Three traditions have emerged for me when my sons married; (1) I would pay for the rehearsal dinner, (2) I made certain there was an open bar at the wedding and (3) I gave the wedding blessings. I always enjoyed writing the blessings because it was my chance to publicly extend my personal wishes, values and hopes to my sons and their new lifelong partners. Nevertheless, I was always nervous about giving the blessings. It seems so ironic that I can make a wonderful living speaking publicly to strangers, but I can be so nervous speaking in front of my own family. Everything is different with our families. Perhaps this is why we are so patient with other people's children. Our own children are more polite to their friends' parents than they are to us! Why do we spend all day being wonderful to strangers and when we come home we are all too often abrupt to the very people who love us? How many times do we actively listen to customers, strangers or casual acquaintances at work; only to come home, drop our bag in the corner and plop ourselves down in our favorite chair? When somebody we love comes up to us and asks, "How did your day go?" how many times do we abruptly respond with, "Please leave me alone. I am so tired and I am afraid that you would not understand what I have been through today!" So, it does not surprise me that the very thing I do professionally would be a stressor to me when I do exactly the same thing in front of my family at my sons' weddings. I recall being reluctant applying for administrative positions in the schools. Ironically, I did not feel comfortable speaking in front of adults. I recall getting a C- as a grade in a public speaking class at Springfield College. The professor told me to be happy with the C- grade because it was a gift. I am sure that she did not mean I was doing it particularly well. Now you know why I am a firm believer in the notion that people are capable of change. One of my sons was arrested in college for urinating in public and using his brother's ID at a local bar. He is now a part-time local police officer in a Cape Cod community. Another of my sons dropped out of high school, used steroids and was arrested for driving an unregistered motor vehicle. He has since graduated with honors with a Bachelors Degree in Exercise Physiology and is currently enrolled in a prestigious nursing program in Boston. Another of my sons was expelled from his college dormitory for his boisterous verbal arguments with his girlfriend. He has since graduated with a Masters degree at Boston College, was the program director for a school made up of high school students that no public high school wants, and is about to establish a private counseling practice. God knows what else they did that Dad never found out about! Let us be honest. How many things did we do that our parents to this day do not know about? Yes, people do change. Be patient with everyone. That includes the people you love. I am convinced that if you do the right things and wait long enough, they will come back. While you may feel that your "ship is sinking," stay on the deck! You cannot throw life preservers to people if you are in the water with them. While the Titanic sank after accidentally hitting the iceberg, some people actually aim at their icebergs, hit them, and then complain about the weather as they sink. Remember, even though the Titanic sank, 711 passengers or 32% of the total number of passengers survived the tragedy! I am including the following blessings that I wrote and shared at my sons' weddings. I am including them because I believe that my wishes project to my sons the kinds of values that most parents wish for their children. In the context of what you have already read, my hopes for my boys should make eminent sense to you.

To Karen and Brian, dated October 25, 1996, and is entitled

"Live"

Live like you mean it.

Live like you are having a blast.

Live every minute.

Live with someone who adores you.

Live with laughter.

Live amongst friends.

Live without a pager.

Live near a park.

Live to enjoy your grandchildren.

Live far from closed minds.

Live without 500 channels.

Live strong

Live safe.

Live healthy.

Live your life, not someone else's.

Live as if today is all there is.

To Andrew and Vikki, September 21, 2001.

Being the Dad of Andy, I have been known on occasion to nag him. This is my last chance to give him some nags in front of an audience. My nags to Andy on his wedding day:

Andy, don't drink too much, you'll pay for it tomorrow!

Don't look for a Gold's Gym in Bermuda.

Don't lose your wallet.

Stop using my good towels to polish the Nova.

Tell Vikki every day that you love her.

Stay out of those tanning beds or you will be itchy throughout

your Bermuda

cruise.

Don't forget to leave your tuxedo with me so I can return it

tomorrow.

Take a moment today to think about Papa and Dzadeau.

Don't lose your driver's license.

Save a dance for Nana and Babci.

When you return from your cruise, finish your internship with

Healthtrax.

Graduate from Bridgewater if for no other reason than to stop

getting parking

tickets from the Campus Police.

Thank Vikki's Mom and Dad.

Give Mom a kiss.

Don't lose your inhaler.

Pray that Brian doesn't drink so much tonight that he grabs the

microphone and sings

Piano Man again.

Tell your Dad that he looks much too young to have sons

approaching 30 and

two grandchildren.

Thank God for his many blessings including Colin, Makayla

and all of his family

and friends gathered here today who love you both very much

and wish you

every happiness forever.

To Jeffrey and Jill, June 10, 2004.

"Good evening, may I have your attention please? A tradition has emerged in my family. When my sons get married, I am given the opportunity to give what has evolved into a non-traditional blessing. Typically, this blessing has been a last minute opportunity for me to give some advice to my sons. Before I get to that, I have a few comments regarding tomorrow's wedding.   Clearly, this wedding was destiny. When Jeffrey came home from the hospital, Judi and I brought our bundle of joy home to his house on Country Way. Years later, this young man is going to make his vows in his spiritual home, also on a road named Country Way. When Jill told her Dad that she was dating a man named Jeffrey Bossio, Dr. Serino reached into his wallet and pulled out a Norm Bossio Enterprise business card. Virtually 15 years ago I spoke at many conference meetings for a man named John Flynn. While I call John my friend, Jill calls him Uncle. Further proof that this wedding was destined is the fact that the entire country considers tomorrow a national day of mourning, while we celebrate the union of Jeff and Jill. During times of celebration, it is traditionally a time to give thanks. My advice to Jeffrey is to give thanks to the following:"

To God: For your health, for Colin, Makayla and all the grandchildren, and for the perfect weather.

To Dr. and Mrs. Serino: For the absolutely perfect wedding.

To Pastor Steve: For his patience with us during the rehearsal.

To Papa: For always making you feel like you were his favorite.

To Nana: For just showing up.

To Andy: For showing up on time.

To Mom: For holding you up and leading when dancing with you tomorrow and for doing so without you even knowing it.

To Carolyn: For being my guest so I do not have to sit alone and walk down the aisle with Vikki again.

To John Flynn: For not singing tomorrow and remembering to speak slowly and loudly.

To the entire Serino Family and the Church: For adopting you personally and spiritually.

Finally.....To Jill: For making you the happiest and luckiest man in the world.

Chapter 17: Life Lessons

I am convinced that we all teach life lessons. Whether we intend to promote our values by proactively spreading our ideals, or simply and quietly going through our lives demonstrating our beliefs in less obvious ways, people are always learning from us.

I have a professional colleague named Joanie, who is a classic example of a person wanting to "give back" to others. She is passionately driven to use her work as a relationship coach, human behavior consultant, and professional speaker to promote healthy lifestyles, wellness and personal joy to others. She has put her vision into action. She broadcasts a weekly "Happy Wednesday" message to over 30,000 listeners, she is putting together a multiple CD/journal to help her clients put her top 40 broadcasts into action plans, and she is currently beginning the process of sponsoring a Habitat for Humanity women built house for a qualified single mother. There is nothing subtle about Joanie's values. She is passionate, proactive, and driven to pursue her clear vision of helping others.

There are, however, other ways of teaching values that are not as obvious. Occasionally, Brian, Karen, Colin, Makayla, and I go to a local resort for the weekend. Since it is generally nearby, it is a convenient way to get away without a great deal of planning and packing. We usually pick a hotel with an indoor and outdoor pool, a game room, and room service. In the evening, Brian and Karen typically go out for the night, while the kids and I order room service. We usually spread out a blanket and make it feel like a little "late night indoor picnic." This past summer, we were at the Seacrest Hotel in Falmouth, MA. After spending a busy day in the pool, feeding endless amounts of quarters into any machine in the game room with a slot, and bluffing the kids into seeing who can get into their pajamas first (I am wondering how much longer that one is going to work!), it is now time to order room service. The kids ordered their usual pizza, chicken fingers, French fries and the largest ice cream sundaes available. After a short while, room service arrived. I opened the door and I was met by a tall black man pushing a cart with our food. I yelled to the kids, "Colin, Makayla, our food is here!" The tall black man came in and said, "What is that little boy's name?" He seemed theatrically surprised. Colin blurted out, "My name is Colin!" The room service man walked over and showed Colin his nametag. Colin read the tag and announced, "Grampa, his name is Colin too!" The tall black man was so nice to the kids. Makayla loves it when somebody notices and mentions how beautiful she is. His manner was gentle and attentive to the kids. After several minutes of gentle banter, I signed the bill and the tall black man left. We ate dinner, the kids wore their desserts and after the standard long stories without endings, the kids fell asleep. The next morning, we met Brian and Karen downstairs in the large dining room for breakfast. Makayla and Colin started telling Mommy and Daddy about the room service. I noticed off to the left side, all the waiters were standing next to the buffet table. There were about ten waiters, all Caucasian, and in the middle was the tall black fellow named Colin. I nudged Colin under the table and pointed over to the clump of waiters standing by the buffet. Colin said excitedly, "Mommy, Daddy, there he is! Over there!" Daddy asked Colin, "Which one is he?" Colin responded without hesitation, "He's right over there Daddy. He is the tall man in the middle!" I hugged Colin. He has no idea about discrimination, civil rights, affirmative action or equal opportunity. I just looked at Brian and Karen, smiled and nodded my head. Then, I hugged two angels.

When I go to the beach with the kids, we always bring French fries for the seagulls. We also bring crackers for the ducks if we happen to be close to a pond or a lake. There is something about feeding animals that kids just love. Makayla always feeds the little seagulls first. She makes an effort to seek out the smallest seagulls and she is careful that they get to eat the French fries first. She says, "The big seagulls are bullies and they take the food away from the little ones!" She says that it is unfair that the big gulls do this. Additionally, the kids carefully dole out the crackers so the baby ducks get fed first. Colin and Makayla witnessed the aggressive seagulls and ducks attempting to take all the food. Kids have a remarkable sense of fairness. They learn early what is fair and unfair. Do you know that public high schools are now generating and implementing "bullying" curriculum? If two toddlers understand the notion of fairness as it applies to sea gulls and ducks, why is it necessary to actually teach why bullying, hazing, and other inappropriate aggressive behaviors are unacceptable in high schools? What happens between the first moments of life when a baby wraps its little hand around anyone's finger to the moment when high school students are gunning down classmates in the school hallways? I have a theory. I believe that kids are shooting each other at schools because adults are shooting each other at work. Kids will not do anything we tell them to do. However, I believe that they will imitate everything we do. No high school student invented the phrase "Going postal." "Road rage" was not a high school invention. I do not believe that it was a high school student who blew up a federal building in Oklahoma City. I think I know what is wrong with kids. They are just like us.

One day, Makayla was having one of her patented "meltdowns." Karen was trying to get Makayla to lie back so she could get her pull-ups and pajamas on. Makayla was having none of it. She was screaming, kicking her legs and generally resisting all of her frustrated Mommy's efforts. The harder Karen tried, the more Makayla resisted. Colin was quietly watching all of this. Colin asked, "Mommy, can I try?" Karen figured since she could not get Makayla to cooperate, why not let Colin try? Immediately, Makayla stopped fussing. She lay back and let Colin put on her pull-ups and uneventfully, smoothly and gracefully put on her pajamas. Impressed, but bewildered, Karen asked Colin, "How did you do it?" Colin took a deep breath and casually explained, "Mommy, sometimes all Makayla needs is a little love and affection." Move over Dr. Phil, a 5-year-old is waiting in the wings.

Youngsters learn to read faster if they love books. Reading stories to young children is the most effective way to assure literacy. We argue as professionals which form of grouping enhances learning, heterogeneous or homogenous grouping. Is it better to teach phonetically or to use a more sight vocabulary approach? Which basal reading program is the best? Perhaps we are over thinking all of this. Kids do things they love. Colin went into first grade basically reading. He did so because Karen read to him virtually every night before he went to bed.

On Easter Sunday morning, Colin called me on the telephone to tell me that Don had given him a Red Sox poster for Easter. Don is a close friend of Brian who is in the alcohol distribution business. Don lives in New Hampshire and he has easy access to Red Sox, Patriots and other major league sports items. Colin was so proud of his new Red Sox poster. He explained to me that the poster had Trot Nixon, Jason Varitek, Curt Shilling, Pedro Martinez, the World Series Trophy, and some words on it. I asked Colin if the words said that the Red Sox were the World Series champions. Colin said he did not know because the poster was upstairs. I asked Colin to go get the poster so he could read the words. Excitedly, he came back in a few moments to tell me that he had the poster. I asked Colin to take a deep breath, focus on the first letter and make that letter sound out loud. Then I said, "Add one of those vowel sounds onto that sound that you just made with your lips, look at the picture, and read what the poster is telling you." In just a few seconds, Colin excitedly said, "I have it Grampa! I know what it says!" I responded, "Tell me!" Colin slowly and deliberately sounded it out. It says, "Bud Light." Even literacy apparently has its price to pay. Be careful what you ask for.

I recall having a short respite one week in my September speaking schedule by virtue of having the Friday off. September is generally extremely busy for me, and this particular week I had been doing a good deal of traveling. It was Thursday afternoon and my mind set was already in a weekend mode. My cell phone rang and it was Brian informing me that he had just booked a last minute job for the next day at a fairly local high school. He told me that the job was going to be for approximately 900 high school students in the gymnasium during the last hour of the day immediately prior to the Friday bus dismissal. He further informed me that I was doing this job pro bono. I am embarrassed to recall the degree to which I started to whine. Brian told me that the nature of the event was a Hurricane Katrina fund raiser. I had a vision of 900 high school kids squirming in the gym bleaches on a Friday afternoon waiting for the dismissal bell to ring while a short bald guy in a suit was standing in the middle of the gym barking into a hand-held microphone messages of "giving up a Friday night pizza to help families in New Orleans put their lives back together." Open gymnasiums do not have the same acoustics as a performing arts center. A huge bucket was going to be placed in the middle of the gymnasium with me, so that the students could file past and place their contributions in it on their way to the buses. At best, this venue was going to be challenging. At worst, I could foresee some rebel sophomore protected by his anonymity shout out, "You suck!" from the safe haven of some distant back row bleacher seat. In any case, the prospect of my three day weekend had been reduced to wishful thinking. I was now resigned to the fact that not only will I be speaking on Friday, but that it will be with a tough audience in a challenging venue for an important cause. It will be hard to convince a gymnasium filled with 900 high school students, whose hormones are raging, to fill the donation bucket with their weekend spending money. However, when Brian books them, I do them. We never shop for jobs. If I am available and Brian successfully negotiates a fee, then we book the date. Apparently the high school principal agreed with Brian's generous offer to book his Dad for no charge. To be fair to Brian, it would be hypocritical for me to try to convince my audience to contribute if I were going to skim an honorarium off the fund raising event proceeds.

As days we dread often do, Friday came quickly. I drove to the high school and looked for the reserved spot for Mr. Bossio at the rear of the building outside the loading dock. A custodian was having a cigarette and apparently waiting for my arrival. After confirming that I was the anticipated speaker, the custodian gave me some ominous advice. He said, "You must be nuts! Do you have any idea what you are about to do?" I simply smiled, thanked him for his help, and thought to myself, "What am I doing here?" I recall two adults walking past me in the hallway. They appeared to be two teachers. While both made eye contact with me, neither one of them said hello or acknowledged me in any way. Moments later, three male students by their lockers noticed me. They wore baggy jeans worn so low that one could only thank God that they were wearing sweatshirts that hung low enough to hide any unwelcome visuals. Each had at least one earring, their hair was spiked and one had at least two tattoos emblazoned on his wrists. At the risk of sounding my age, they looked like they were ready to go trick or treating. The moment they made eye contact with me, they came right over to me and said, "Hello Sir, are you looking for the main office?" Startled by the wonderfully refreshing hospitality, I said, "Yes, thank you for asking." Then they offered to accompany me through the maze of halls to the main lobby. I found it ironic that the first real welcome to the school was from kids, not adults.

The principal greeted me enthusiastically. I have such a wonderful job. When I arrive in venues, people are always so relieved that the speaker actually showed up. I do not remember such animated greetings when I showed up as a school principal. The program was described to me. It was simple, yet elegant. The entire school filed into the gym in an incredibly organized fashion accompanied by the solemn music of a nationally ranked student bagpipe player. The elegance of the bagpipes added an exquisite touch to the usual "pep rally" tone generally associated with Friday afternoon assemblies in the gymnasium. It was now time for my introduction. The president of the student class read my introduction, and I was somewhat amazed with two things: (1) I was relieved to hear that the microphone actually worked. You might be surprised at how many do not, and (2) The 900 students were actually listening. In fact, they were wonderfully attentive, responsive and appreciative of my efforts throughout the entire presentation. I fed off their energy. There is something refreshingly honest about talking to high school students. If they like you, they will let you know. I have a sense that if they do not like you, they would also let you know. The hour flew by for me. It was almost magical. At the end of my speech (I am using that term loosely here), they were generous in their efforts to let me know how much they enjoyed my work. After speaking, I shook the hand of the appreciative principal and I headed out quickly so I could avoid the rush of all the school buses. I secretly hoped that I would get to see the custodian on my way out the door. I did not.

When I arrived home, there was a message on my telephone answering machine. It was the principal of the high school I just left. He sounded almost giddy. After my speech, the students actually put $6,500.00 in the huge bucket on the way out and ultimately contributed $9,600.00 to the Katrina Hurricane Relief Fund. I was stunned. I learned a number of important issues from this speaking engagement.

1. The future of our country is in good hands.

2. Even kids with baggy pants, earrings and tattoos can be generous and sensitive to the needs of others.

3. Again, my expectations were wrong.

4. Today's high school students will be tomorrow's teachers, principals, fireman, lawyers, judges, doctors, nurses, politicians, and world leaders for my grandchildren.

5. Sometimes Brian is absolutely right.

6. Whining is self-serving.

7. On a Friday afternoon before bus dismissal, sitting in the bleachers of a crowded gymnasium, 900 kids can teach an old principal a lot of important life lessons.

Chapter 18: Pygmalion: The Self-fulfilling Prophecy

One of the most interesting notions about the self-fulfilling prophecy is the fact that you are usually right. If you truly believe that you are capable of doing something, you have automatically enhanced your chances for success. Conversely, however, if you believe in your heart that you are incapable of doing something, you have immediately diminished your chances for success. Either way, you are right! It would appear that our own attitude has a major impact on our accomplishments. Perhaps it is time to review our own expectations.

I have been asked a number of times which of the thousands of speaking engagements I have had, since I started in 1980, was the most memorable. I have had many. I have had Stephen King, Bill Clinton (when he was governor in Arkansas), state governors, big city mayors and even a remote Indian village tribunal in British Columbia as audience members. I once spoke in Waco, TX after the Branch Davidian tragedy, addressed thousands in the Hoosier Dome and keynoted a dinner meeting with 45 nuclear physicists. I once keynoted the Argentina Bank Marketers Association in Buenos Aires. I was the only person in the room who spoke English. Every audience member had a headset and heard my words through a translator. It was awkward to hear the audience laugh about 7 seconds after I said something. They must have missed a lot of what I said because less than two months after I spoke to them, the entire banking system collapsed in Argentina. Yes, they paid me in cash. My only point here is that I have had a lot of memorable jobs over the 26 years that I have been speaking publicly. However, there is one engagement that I would consider to be among the most interesting.

In 1989, I was contracted to speak in Charleston, SC at the Omni Hotel. Charleston is such a romantic and historic city with lots of southern charm. Elegant retail stores, Spanish moss hanging from the trees, and obvious southern hospitality, all combined to make Charleston a great place for an annual national conference. However, this conference was going to be interesting, if not intriguing. I was contracted to be the keynote speaker at the 89th Annual Meeting of the National Concrete Burial Vaults Association. My expectations kicked in. What kind of people would make cement burial vaults for a living? Why would they meet once a year? What would they talk about when they got there? So, I flew to Charleston early enough to arrive the night before my speech. I like to wake up in the state where I am speaking. I also like to further prepare for my speech by reviewing the agenda, seeing the actual venue, and perhaps getting an anonymous peek at my audience. I expected to see a bunch of people humped over like the Hunchback of Notre Dame. I was a bit intrigued as to what the vendor exhibition hall was going to look like. Can you imagine being a vendor at these trade association meetings? I could not imagine making my living by giving out key chains! After checking into the Omni Hotel, I took a walk to see the vendors' exhibits. It was macabre. One exhibitor actually gave out baseball caps with embroidered caskets on them! My expectations were being reinforced. This is going to be an odd group.

That night, I reviewed the conference agenda in my room. Much to my surprise, there was a pre-conference breakout session that was going to be held in the grand ballroom. I will go. They will have no idea who I am. I will wear blue jeans and I will simply sit inconspicuously in the back of the room. I never wear nametags. Usually, speaker nametags have red ribbons hanging down to the floor. You can always tell how important conference participants are by the number of colored ribbons hanging off their nametags. I sneaked into the grand ballroom, and I will never forget what I saw and heard next.

Approximately 300 people (no hunchbacks that I could see!) were sitting under a huge chandelier with a man standing in front of them with an overhead projector. He was wearing a black suit. I expected that. He had black shoes. I expected that as well. He wore black socks and a black tie, and a dark shirt to offset the entire outfit.

I could not believe what I heard this man say to the group. Remember, I was there, so I am not making this up! He was bemoaning the fact that last year, the death rate had dipped to 1.9 million deaths annually. He said, however, and optimistically, "With a little bit of luck, this year the numbers might bounce back to the 2.3 million deaths we enjoyed last year." I could not believe my ears! I felt like yelling out, "You must be kidding here!" Nevertheless, let me tell you something about the conference attendees. They were absolutely wonderful! They were so much fun. Most of the businesses were family owned and they were in the industry for generations. I stayed up with them all night after my morning speech. We laughed, partied, and drank all night. It could have been formaldehyde for all I know. My expectations were wrong. They were professional business people in an industry that very few of us understand. I thoroughly enjoyed my time with them and I learned a lot about their work. I also learned to be careful with my own expectations.

How do you feel when somebody prefaces what they say with, "You are not going to like what I am about to tell you!" or "Are you sitting down for this news?" My guess is that you brace yourself for bad news. Your expectations were established before you even knew what was going to be said. "May I see you in my office? Please bring your policy handbook with you. You may want to hire an attorney to represent you." Again, our expectations would be such that there certainly would not be any good coming out of this meeting. Remember, you have no news yet and already you feel defensive. Already you would have negative feelings and negative expectations for what is about to happen. Students who are assigned to teachers they do not like, are not likely to do well in their classes. Conversely, teachers' expectations for students' abilities absolutely affect achievement and rates of learning. Expectations are that powerful! I once had a luncheon speech booked in the Pocono Mountains at a place called the Split Rock Resort. Since it was a luncheon meeting, I had to get dressed in my suit and leave at an ungodly hour for an early morning commuter flight out of Boston Logan Airport. When I boarded the Park and Fly van, the driver said, "Good morning sir! Where are you heading today?" When I left the van, she wished me a wonderful day. She projected lots of energy as she attentively and courteously engaged me. When I tried to lug my briefcase and overnight bag through the terminal revolving doors, a man came rushing over to assist me. "Let me help you with that sir." It was amazing to me that I was being treated so well so early in the morning. After the sales associate gave me a bagel and coffee at the coffee shop near my gate, she offered, "Here is your receipt sir for your business trip." Clearly, I was enjoying the various courtesies being offered to me. I gave my luncheon speech at the resort.

The next day, I was contracted to speak at a dinner event in Lawrence, KS. Since it was late at night the next day, I was able to take a mid-morning flight to Kansas. As a result, I did not wear my suit to the airport. I wore jeans, sneakers, an old windbreaker, a Boston Red Sox hat, and I did not shave. How many people said, "Good-morning sir?" How many people at the airport offered me assistance through the revolving doors at the airport? Do you think the vendors were concerned that I have a receipt for all my "business trip expenditures?" What was the difference? I am absolutely convinced that the suit made all the difference in the world. Perhaps people's expectations change depending on what we are wearing.

Anybody who travels for a living will testify how differently they are treated at airports depending on what they are wearing. Evidently clothing changes people's expectations.

Notice how we speak to people who do not speak English as their primary language. Generally, we speak more loudly and clearly. What if I walked through a public facility and I had a special need for which I would require reasonable accommodation? What if I were a single parent obviously being overwhelmed by my five screaming, disruptive, and raucous children? Would I be treated differently? Apparently not only do our expectations affect our behavior, but they also seem to affect the behavior of others.

When I was a school principal, I introduced the notion of an outdoor week long out-of-state camping program for the children and staff. It was a wonderful opportunity for a particular grade level, usually 4th, 5th or 6th grades, to get away for a week with teachers, parent volunteers and, yes, even the principal to develop relationships and bonds that were more substantive than those established during a regular six-hour school day. We would do lots of team building activities requiring parents, teachers, children and staff to work together in collaborative problem solving activities. Learning new songs, sitting together around campfires, and sharing new experiences together had tremendous benefits in terms of enhancing student, staff and community morale. However, as we already discussed, all change can be stressful. Even wonderful, new and exciting changes can cause stress to people addicted to routines and past practice. While most parents thought it was a great idea (Some verbalized how wonderful it would be to have a full week without their kids.), smaller groups of parents felt that the weeklong trip to New Hampshire was too long, the kids were too young, and the program was not academic enough. My job was to now market the new idea emphasizing, of course, why the experience would be good for their children. I scheduled an evening informational meeting for parents.

At the meeting, I showed slides of smiling children and adults working together in productive teams helping each other squeeze through hanging tires, climbing over padded walls, catching each other blindly falling backwards into the supportive arms of their teammates, and generally marketing the experience as having a wide variety of positive consequences for everyone. I assured the parents that we would have a nurse with us at all times, that the food would be nutritious, and that the adult/child ratio would assure a safe and secure experience for every child. I emphasized that we would be integrating the camping experiences with our curriculum. For those parents anxious about the "no work, all play" risks of letting a child live at a campsite for a week, I made it very clear that we would vigorously integrate curriculum content into all program activities of the camping experience. I also made it clear to the parents how important it would be for me to know if any child had a medical consideration that we would need to know about before leaving for the trip. We would make certain to attend to any medical condition as long as we were advised about it. I realized that my primary responsibility would be the health and safety of every student 24 hours per day. I invited any parent with such concerns to see me after the meeting and I would be happy to discuss any matter in this regard.

After the meeting, a reticent looking Mom wanted to talk to me. She said that her son does not want to go on the trip, despite the fact that she thought he could really benefit from it. She said, "He has a medical problem. He is a bed-wetter. Can you help?" I said, "Of course, I can. Trust me. I will make sure he will be taken care of in a way that will be confidential and secure."   Reassured, the Mom thanked me and she informed me that her son was going to go on the trip with us.

The big day finally came. It was a Monday morning and we were heading to New Hampshire. I assigned the "bed-wetter" to my seat on the bus so we could spend some time together. I assigned him to my cabin. I even assigned him to my bunk, the bottom bunk of course; there is no reason to be stupid here. The first night, I woke the little boy up at about 2:00 a.m. I figured if he and I went to the lavatory together in the middle of night, I would enhance the possibility that he would awaken dry the next morning. Heck, I figured I would wake up dry too. I gently shook him. Groggily, he woke. Without asking why, he crawled out of the bunk and followed me through the woods to the lavatory facility. Without a word being said, we stood there peeing together. Oh my! Talk about bonding! We walked back to the cabin and he crawled back into his bunk. I said, "Good night" and he responded, "Good night Mr. B." The next morning when we woke up, I checked in with the boy. I asked him if everything was okay. He said that he was fine. I discreetly reminded him that I had spoken with his mother and that it would be okay for him to confide in me. He stated vigorously, "I am fine, Mr. B!" I insisted, "I am here to help. Please, tell me if everything is okay." He defensively insisted, "Mr. B, everything is great!" However, he was dry as a bone, and I was so pleased.

The next night, the same scenario emerged. At 2:00 a.m., I woke him up and without comment he got up, followed me to the lavatory, we peed, we walked back to the cabin, and I tucked him in. We exchanged good night wishes and slept. The next morning, I discreetly checked in with him again, asking the same questions in as many different ways as I could. He insisted that he was fine. I even sensed that he was becoming increasingly irritated as I pursued the line of questioning. However, his sheets were absolutely dry. I am doing it. I am keeping my promise. He remained dry as a bone. Throughout the entire week he remained absolutely dry. Four nights and five days, he was dry. It was now Friday afternoon and we were heading home. As we entered the school's circular driveway, the kids were singing. The foul smell of dirty clothes permeated the bus, and I spotted the Mom anxiously awaiting the little boy's return. I stepped off the bus and briskly walked over to the Mom. I assured her that everything was fine. "We had a perfect week! There were no problems at all!" The little boy was hugging his Mom and he agreed that it was a great week. The Mom thanked me for all I did, for my leadership, for introducing the camping experience to the school, and for returning the children back home safely. I modestly replied, "You are perfectly welcome." I then mustered up my "Mr. Bossio hunk voice" and retorted, "It is my job." Then, I could feel the energy beginning to muster up inside me. I could not stand it any longer and I blurted out, "He was dry as a bone!" Quizzically, the Mom said, "Huh?" I repeated, in a somewhat more measured tone, "Well, you know.... He was dry as a bone!" Looking at her face, I felt a sick feeling run through my entire body. Oh my God! I had awakened the wrong kid! My expectations were wrong. Check out your expectations. If you do not, you may regret it. Can you imagine? In some other cabin, a little boy in another bunk had an absolutely miserable week because Mr. Bossio did not double check his expectations.

Chapter 19: How to Deal with Difficult People

This chapter will address, explore and discuss specific approaches to managing conflict inside and outside the work and family domains. I am including my 10 tips to strategically deal with difficult people. A variety of communication issues involving giving and receiving feedback, dealing with conflict, giving clear and concise messages, and recognizing assertive, non-assertive, passive-aggressive, manipulative and other modes of behavior that tend to affect both our relationships, and our collaborative approaches to problem solving will be covered. The basic issue of dealing with difficult people would appear to be communication. Whether it be unclear, misdirected, untrue, unfair or not enough of it, communication is often the key to dealing with anybody. Children learn to communicate (or not communicate) by modeling behavior. Speech itself is learned from mimicking. Modes and patterns of speech characterize not only languages, but regions and nationalities.

An example of dysfunctional communication can be illustrated by the following caricature: A husband and wife are lying in bed together as the 11 o'clock news appears on the television. Neither person is talking because both are reading a magazine or newspaper. It is late, it is dark, they are both on their own sides of the bed, and nobody is fighting. It does not get much better than that. Suddenly, one person (it does not matter which one) starts clipping his fingernails. Long white curly nails are flying all over the sheets. The other person thinks, "Yuck! What a disgusting thing to do!" The person cutting the fingernails notices the look of contempt in his partner's face and asks, "Honey, are you upset about anything? Are you okay?" Honey answers, "No, of course not. I am fine." Be aware of people who describe their state of being as "fine." "Fine" is often a codeword for "I do not feel like telling you how I really feel." In any case, the partner who has denied being upset by the flying fingernails notes to herself to be sure to write the annoying behavior in the "secret lists" in her journal. Relieved to hear that cutting fingernails is not upsetting, the offending partner moves on to cutting toenails. It is so important that we communicate directly with the person who needs to hear the message. How many times do spouses complain about each other to neighbors? Note how many times people talk about other people. The entire school community is particularly guilty of this. Parents talk about teachers. Teachers talk about parents. We all talk about children. Everyone talks about the principal. Principals talk about the superintendent. Superintendents talk about school committees. The ironic part of these communication misdirects is the fact that the field of education is basically made up of systems of communication. If any institution ought to be good at communication, it should be one that educates young people. One of my pet peeves as school principal was always the reluctance of some parents to direct their comments, questions or concerns to us, rather than to friends and neighbors. After all, we are in the best position to address their concerns. One could argue that if we do not direct our concerns directly to the person who needs to hear the message, we are actually denying that person the opportunity to do something about it. If after confronting the person directly with our concerns, they do not do anything about it, then it can be argued that now we would have more to talk about. If someone's behavior deserves our concern, I would argue that the offending person has the right to know it. If we deny them that right, we are in no position to talk about them. If a parent feels that a teacher is assigning too much homework, the teacher has a right to know it. If the parent tells the teacher, the teacher has three choices. He can explain the homework policy, continue to assign the same amount of homework, or reduce the amount of homework assigned. If the teacher is not confronted with the homework concern, there would be no reason for the amount of homework assigned to change. In this same regard, if you do not want your partner to cut toenails in bed, then tell him that cutting fingernails in bed bothers you.

We are as guilty of this within the school. If a particular music teacher is guilty of calling in sick virtually every Monday, the teacher who has music scheduled on Monday morning is likely to be very unhappy. Unfortunately, however, the teacher would more likely complain in the teachers' lounge to whomever is there, rather than confront the music teacher directly. After all, if the music teacher calls in sick on Mondays, the classroom teacher will miss the free period every Monday morning. After a certain length of time of this frustration, the classroom teacher makes an appointment to tell the principal. Upon entering the office, the teacher says, "Mr. Bossio, I am going to tell you something about the music teacher, but I do not want you to do anything about it. If you do, she will know that I told you." If I had a nickel for every time I heard a sentence like that, I would be a very rich man! One option the principal has, of course, is to respond, "Well, if you don't want me to do anything about this, then don't tell me." However, since principals are merely teachers who are promoted by God, we are subject to the same foibles. I would like to think, however, that principals would not generally participate in talking behind teachers' backs in the lounge. We have a special technique to communicate with staff. We send out a memo. Of course, it is addressed to ALL STAFF and reads something like this: "It has been brought to my attention that certain patterns of attendance are denying certain teachers the benefits of regularly scheduled planning periods as a result of certain specialists periodically calling in sick." How is that for directness? Of course, the whole school reads it, except for one teacher because it was sent out on Monday. Read this chapter with an open mind. A pre-requisite for this chapter will be a sense of humor. Warning....this content may hit very close to home.

For the purposes of this chapter, it may be helpful for me to distinguish the difference between "conflict resolution" and "conflict management." I believe that conflict resolution is rare. How many times have you heard someone say, "You're right, I'm wrong, I will change?" Conflict resolution presumes closure. Closure is rare in conflict. An example would be a husband and wife arguing about religion. The discussion escalates to a major fight lasting several days. Conflict resolution would involve one party to give up and simply change religions. Conflict management, on the other hand, would be a more simple, "Honey, every time we talk about religion, we have a major fight. Can we agree tonight that we not talk about religion?" Nobody wins, nobody loses. The parties have simply agreed to manage their conflict by not talking about what ends up to be a volatile topic for them. I believe that it is more realistic for us to begin to find ways to manage conflict situations as they arise, as opposed to trying to resolve all of them. In this regard, let us begin to explore my 10 tips to deal with the difficult people in our lives.

1.   __You cannot deal with irrational people rationally.__ __Do not argue with people.__

It is fine to disagree with people. That is healthy. Agree to disagree if you must. But, arguments risk the "sulking period" that follows. Sulking can only be dysfunctional. Nothing is more self-serving than a period of time when we avoid talking. Remaining upstairs, while your partner is downstairs, is not going to help manage your differences. Hearing footsteps on the stairs, sends you scurrying to appear busy and pre-occupied. That is why arguing in a car is very difficult. Where are you going to go? While the car is moving straight ahead, both of you are looking out the side windows. Not only is that emotionally alienating, but it is outright dangerous! One of the additional problems of sulking is the impending, "Who is going to give in first?" scenario. Usually it is the same slushball who tends to make the first conciliatory advances. How frustrating is it when you ask your partner, "Are you angry?" Despite the long face and sullen demeanor, the response is simple. "I am fine." It would appear that men and women may have different agendas during these kinds of interactions. The man just wants her to say what she is really thinking. The woman is vexed because if he really loves her, he would already know and he would not have to ask. Generally, there is very little return on the investment required to argue with people. Rational discourse to irrational behavior will simply not work. Avoid the temptation to overwhelm irrational behavior with logic and reason.

2.   Separate feelings from behaviors.

Feelings are always legitimate. Behavior may or may not be appropriate. When Andy was younger, he was always afraid of thunderstorms. Whenever he woke up at night with thunder and lightening, he would jump out of bed, run down the hallway and jump into my bed unannounced. I had two choices as to how I would respond. I could have said to Andy, "Get back to bed, stop crying and stop acting like a baby!" If I had responded in that way, I would not have recognized his legitimate feelings of fear; indeed terror of the thunderstorm. Sending him back to his bed and calling him a baby because he was in tears was to deny him his very real feelings. On the other hand, I could have said to Andy, "I understand how you feel. Thunderstorms can certainly be scary. I am also sometimes startled when I hear an unexpected clap of thunder and every once in awhile, lightening can start fires and do tremendous damage, but gee, Andy, 18 years old is kind of old to be jumping into my bed unannounced!" Do you hear the difference? While his fear is absolutely legitimate, his behavior may not be acceptable. Separating feelings and behaviors help us understand difficult people. Telling somebody that "they should not feel that way" is not only unproductive, it can be resented. Fear, guilt, anger, jealousy and other emotions are real and part of our being human. Behavior, however, can involve propriety, judgment, and skill set. Understanding feelings gives us a more holistic view of behavior. And as such, this more expansive perspective brings me to my next tip.

3.   **Pick your battles.**

Not everything has to be a crisis. Any of you who have raised children through adolescence understand this concept very well. If you do not pick your battles with teenagers, you will go crazy. Ever have a major argument with an adolescent? They tend to involve a lot of anger, frustration, and words that neither party intended to say. For those of you who answered in the affirmative to the question about having an argument with an adolescent, I invite you to go back and re-read suggestion #1 above on my list of tips to deal with difficult people. In any case, let's go back to our confrontation with the adolescent. Now that the impasse is over, both parties are walking away from each other. Suddenly you hear your adolescent adversary say faintly under his breath some very bad words referring to you. Now, you have a choice. Are you going to respond? Or are you going to "not hear" the "somewhat directed" profanity towards you? Your choice includes two simple options. Either begin again your argument or wait until another time when a more obvious display of disrespect is directed at you. I do not have the answer to that question. I only suggest that you consider the options before automatically escalating the volatile situation. Is this battle worth fighting? In some situations, what you do not do may be more important than what you do. Pick a battle that is worth fighting. Some battles are worth fighting even if you lose. When I was a school superintendent, a newly elected school committee member devoted her first meeting to publicly addressing the issue of why we offer chocolate milk to children as a lunch purchase option. She viewed this option as an unhealthy choice. Since I wanted to reserve a public confrontation for a more important issue, I simply suggested that we poll the parents and let the parents decided. The school committee member agreed. The parents voted and we continued the choice of the chocolate milk option. That was simply a battle I did not feel was worth fighting. I saved the public battle for the issues I felt were worth fighting. I will not win every battle. This reality brings me to my next suggestion.

4.   Consider the price for being right.

On occasion, we win an argument and pay dearly for it. There are a lot of people who live all by themselves who were absolutely right. They have the rest of their lives to tell anyone who will listen how right they were. My mother was once in line at a local community bank to do some banking business. Among other transactions, she was making a deposit of some kind. As my mother was standing at the window, she started to fill out the requisite deposit slip. The bank teller interrupted my mother to remind her that the bank policy clearly stated, "Deposit slips are not to be filled out at the window." There was a very convenient table off to the side dedicated to the customers for this purpose. The table was convenient and well lit with pens and every conceivable bank form readily available to the customers. The teller reminded my mother that she was holding up the line. She asked my Mom, "Please complete the deposit slips at the table. Then, get back in line and I will be happy to help you." Yes, the bank teller was right. She was simply enforcing bank policy. She was trained to do this. However, if the teller had simply leaned forward and looked at my Mom more carefully, she might have noticed that my mother had Parkinson's disease and she was working hard at simply holding the pen. When my mother told me that story, my first impulse was to go down to the bank with her, withdraw every dime in her multiple accounts and transfer the money to another bank. That bank nearly lost thousands of dollars that day because one employee had to be right. My Mom apparently was aware of the previous suggestion and convinced me to not pick this battle.

A local pharmacy where I shop almost daily would not let me enlarge a 25 year-old school picture of my son because of a posted copyright law on the machine forbidding customers to do so without written permission from the photographer. I argued that it would be difficult because the photographer was no longer in business. The 2 X 3 class picture was 25 years old and I simply wanted to make one 8 X 10 enlargement. The store manager was technically right, but he forbade me to do so. As a result, I returned the $200.00 worth of merchandise I was going to purchase and I no longer shop at that store. I have also told this story in several local and national venues when I discuss customer service. When I tell the story in public, I mention the store by name. Again, the manager was probably right in terms in technicality. But, in terms of accommodation and service to the customer, I felt alienated. I went to another local pharmacy and they allowed me to make the 8 X 10 enlargement and I now patronize that store for my local convenience store shopping.

5.   **Do not add energy to a confrontation.**

When I was school principal, I began to notice that every year the same teachers would send students to the office for disciplinary action. It did not seem to matter what children were assigned to the class. I could begin to predict which teachers would send children from the class to the office. After awhile, it occurred to me that maybe it was not just the students who were having problems. Why is it that year after year, some teachers never send students out of class, while other teachers were doing so on a daily basis? Announcing to a class on the first day of school, "Vacation is over! I don't want to be here either. I am not going to babysit this year!" is adding enough negative energy into the classroom to virtually assure alienation, confrontation and disruptive behavior. Miserable teachers seem to have miserable students. Fun teachers tend to have fun students. Some people actually find confrontation to be recreational. We all have stories of people who love arguing politics.

One of the biggest nightmares of being a school principal is dealing with a teacher's anger in a confrontation. This anger can manifest itself in situations ranging from irrational punishments to unrealistic expectations. For example, I have had teachers threaten to not let the entire class of children go home until "Somebody admits to spilling the paint" to a bus driver who literally hosed down an entire busload of middle school students (including parent chaperones) at the end of a field trip. Nothing adds more energy to a confrontation than adult anger. Once parental anger becomes part of the confrontation, unreasonable, illogical and irrational punishments often follow. My mother had a way of punishing me as a child that could be considered a classic example in this regard.

While I have absolutely no recollection of what misbehavior warranted my Mom's disciplinary actions, I do recall vividly her anger and her sanctions. I remember wincing as her anger escalated to the point where she would blurt out her punishments. Her stubborn nature would prohibit her from backing off her threat. Once she said it, that was it. There was no going back. Mom had a propensity for taking me out of any organized group in which I was a member. As a result, over the years Mom took me out of little league, cub scouts, drum and bugle corps and even the school safety patrol. The safety patrol one really hurt because I was actually chosen the honor of being the captain, shiny blue badge and all. At the risk of sounding self-serving, I have absolutely no idea what I could have done to warrant such punishments. My sense is that if I can vividly recall the punishments in my mid 50's for misbehavior in my pre-teen years, perhaps the sanctions were disproportionate to the misbehavior. Being an only child with a classic Type A personality, it was important for me to be actively involved in activities involving other children. I recall how much I enjoyed being part of a team, club or organization. It is important for us to make certain that our own anger does not taint the degree to which we respond to children. I find it ironic that we often respond to Type B children by making them join scouts, clubs, little league and other organizations requiring social interactions, while we punish Type A children by taking them out of these activities. My parents did, however, send me to a YMCA camp for eight weeks every summer. I am not certain if they sent me to the camp for me or for them. It also occurs to me that it does not matter. I loved going to Camp Burgess every summer between the ages of 9 and 16 years of age.

The bus driver taking the 7th graders on the field trip clearly overreacted, escalating the problem by adding his own energy in response to the misbehavior of the children. According to the driver, "The kids were acting like animals." This kind of analogy is never a good sign. At the end of the field trip, the driver drove the busload of children, teachers and parent volunteers to the town barn, rather than back to the school. This is another bad sign. The town barn is where the school buses are fueled up, serviced, housed and washed. According to everyone involved (including the bus driver), he drove over to the area where the buses are washed each week. Without saying a word to anybody, he parked the bus, exited the bus, turned on the water faucet, re-entered the bus with a high powered hose nozzle, and hosed down every person inside the bus. Parents, kids and teachers were all screaming as the emergency door flew open and the passengers scrambled for safety. The parents called the police, while the bus driver returned the hose to its appropriate storage hanger. As I recalled the fallout from this incredibly unfortunate incident, the initial misbehavior of the children that prompted the bus driver's response was never even discussed. The bus driver's overreaction overshadowed the misbehavior of the children. Adding unnecessary energy to a problem not only potentially complicates the problem, but it risks losing sight of the original situation that caused the problem in the first place.

Examples of adding energy to confrontation are easy to recognize. They include raising your voice, threatening irrational consequences, adding physicality, demanding specific actions and interjecting anger. Insisting that someone apologize can further complicate what could be a de-escalated confrontation. When one party starts to yell, it prompts the other person to do the same. When both parties are yelling, neither person is listening to the other. Children have a remarkable ability to "tune out" adults who are yelling at them. Interestingly enough, spouses have this same ability.

I once had an irate father make an appointment to see me regarding his 8th grade son's science grade. This physically massive man projected a very threatening image. His imposing stature was impressive. His furious attitude caught everyone's attention (including mine) as he came flying into my office. He refused to sit down, to shake my hand, or to participate in any effort to exchange initial pleasantries. His animation and voice tone suggested that he was not going to add energy to this conference; he was bringing his energy with him. I braced myself for what was sure to be a very unpleasant conference. With an accusatory tone, the father informed me that his son received a grade of "C" from his science teacher. He further informed me that his son had received all A's and B's in his other subjects, and that his C grade in science would jeopardize his candidacy for admission into a prestigious private high school. He had planned on transferring to the private high school for his freshman year if he was, of course, accepted into the highly academically competitive school. Since I knew why the Dad was going to meet with me, I had previously checked with the science teacher. Apparently the boy's test scores averaged 72%, quizzes averaged 66%, he was missing a number of homework assignments and he received a C- for his science project. Clearly, the boy earned his C grade for the semester. I responded to the Dad's tirade by calmly explaining how the teacher arrived at the C grade. Unaffected by my rational and descriptive explanation, the Dad simply reiterated how the C would hurt his son's admission into the private school and that he needed all honor grades to get in. He acted as if he had not heard a word that I said. I again demonstrated that mathematically his son actually earned a low C grade. Not the least bit phased by the facts, the father appeared to be further irritated and became even more animated in his insistence that his son needed an honor grade in science. It was a very tense situation. I sensed that the man was on the verge of losing total control of what little propriety he was exercising. At this point, I took a deep breath and looked into his eyes. I paused and then said, "Okay, here is what I am willing to do. Despite the fact that your son did not earn this, I will speak to his science teacher and see if he is willing to give your son an undeserved B." My comment seemed to startle him. His face softened, his shoulders slouched and he sat down. He looked up at me and almost sadly said to me, "I don't want you to give my son a B." I responded immediately by asking, "Sir, what is it you want?" He hesitated and said in almost a pathetic tone, "I want my son to deserve the B." Relieved and pleased, I suggested that perhaps he needs to pursue this discussion with his son. Clearly, I gambled and successfully defused his energy and, as a result, brought closure to a very unpleasant confrontation.

The most difficult job I ever had was being an assistant principal of a middle school. I was the school disciplinarian. I was convinced that my job was to empty the bench outside my office, while the teachers' job was to fill it. I was assigned, among other supervisory tasks, daily lunchroom duty. All by myself, I would stand in a lunchroom three times per day for increments of 30 minutes each, supervising 6th, 7th and 8th graders eating lunch. I did this for three years, 180 days each year. I recall one day spotting a 7th grader eating lunch wearing a baseball hat. The student handbook clearly states, "Students are not to wear hats in the cafeteria." Ignoring all four of my previous suggestions listed above and surrounded by 150 students eating lunch, I confronted the boy one on one. With my Mr. Bossio voice, I bellowed out, "Please stand!" The entire cafeteria hushed to watch the confrontation. The boy stood up and faced me. Of course, he had to be 6 inches taller than me. Nevertheless, he was wearing a baseball cap, clearly a violation of school policy. I told him that if he did not remove the hat in three seconds, I will be sending him to the office for further disciplinary action. The entire cafeteria responded in unison, "Ooh!" The boy looked into my eyes as I began to count. "One..." Again, the other students were rooting us on. "Two...." The room was filling with tension as the energy of the confrontation in the cafeteria heightened.

Remember, only moments ago, everyone (including the "hat wearing offender"), was eating lunch. Who made this confrontation worse than it needed to be? Who added the unnecessary energy to this confrontation? What were my chances that this 7th grader was going to take his hat off in front of 150 of his classmates? We all know the answers to these questions. While the 7th grader violated the school rule, I was the one who established the confrontation. I would have had much better luck if I had walked up to the boy while he was quietly eating lunch with his friends, put my arms supportively on his shoulder and gently said to him, "Hey, pal, how about taking your hat off? Thanks." I am not saying that this will work every time, but it certainly has a better chance of success than the public confrontation that I set up. Ironically, it would appear that students are not the only people who learn in our schools.

6.   Keep your sense of humor.

I recall once having a 1st grade youngster sent to my office for misbehavior in his class. I do not recall exactly what he did that warranted his banishment from the classroom, but I do remember how angry he made his teacher. Apparently the teacher did not read my suggestion #5 regarding not adding energy to a confrontation. She was going nuts describing this little boy. I recall the teacher's red face, animation, pulsating veins on her neck and forehead, and shrieking allegations. The little boy sat there quietly listening to her accusations. He looked pathetic, but adorable. He had beautiful steely blue eyes, golden blonde hair cut in a fashionable Dutch boy style, fair skin, and his mouth was circled down at the corners as he struggled to resist the obviously impending tears. His lower lip began to protrude and quiver as the teacher pointed her finger in his face. My heart almost broke as two lone tears began to trickle down his pudgy cheeks from his sapphire blue eyes. Since we have already learned from section one in this chapter that you cannot deal with irrational people rationally, I felt that there would be little benefit in dealing with the teacher, at least in her current status of unbridled anger. I turned to the little boy with all of the professionalism, propriety, and dignity I could muster and with my best Mr. Bossio voice, I asked the little boy, "Well now, what do you have to say for yourself?" He looked up at me and said, "Mr. Bossio, I didn't do nothing bad. I was a good boy. I didn't do a f__king thing wrong." I had to immediately turn my chair around and look out the window behind me. There was no way that I was going to maintain any kind of decorum at this point. I asked the teacher to bring the little boy outside to sit on my bench. When she returned, we both started to laugh uncontrollably for what seemed like ten minutes. When we finally regained our composure, we brought the little lad back into my office for a brief Mr. Bossio lecture on the importance of being well behaved and a good listener. The little boy was never sent to my office again. It was apparent that he had learned his lesson. I know, however, that I learned a lesson about the power of laughter. If you are a teacher and you do not have a sense of humor, you are literally in the wrong job. If you are a parent, a sense of humor will be your most effective coping mechanism and survival strategy for dealing with the ongoing challenges and frustrations of parenthood. I have met many people in our schools (including principals) who take themselves much too seriously.

Anyone who has worked anywhere near an elementary school knows two of the most festive holidays are Halloween and Valentine's Day. Both days involve class parties complete with cupcakes, cookies, costumes and assorted other food substances specifically banned in the nutrition unit of our school's health curriculum. It was Valentine's Day when I was returning to my office after floating through the building visiting the children during their parties. I always made a point of at least walking through every class every day. It was a great excuse to get out of my office to avoid all the boring paperwork and to maintain that "Mr. Bossio" visibility in the building. I loved the casual and spontaneous interactions with the children. I had received countless homemade valentines as I returned to the office. Outside my office on the bench was an upper grade student sent to me for an apparent discipline problem. The teacher sent down the sixth grader for fighting during recess. Energized by several Valentine cupcakes, heart-shaped cookies, and God knows how many candied hearts, I started my lecture on fighting. I have little patience for bullying, aggressive behavior, and lack of respect for others. As a result, my comments regarding fighting were well honed. I was standing, articulating, and brandishing my finger to further emphasize the seriousness of the violation. Then, the unthinkable happened. Just as I was to describe the legal implications of fighting (assault and battery), which usually drives home to the older students the potential complications of further violations in this regard, I noticed something beginning to creep out of my shirt sleeve. Of course, rather than ignore it, I stopped and investigated. Much to my horror, it was a homemade red valentine heart with white lace glued on the edge. The student started to laugh. I started to laugh. We both roared. Then, the boy pointed to the back of my suit jacket and said, "Mr. Bossio, look at your back." I took my suit jacket off and saw the ultimate indignity. Some child (hopefully it was a child) put a sticker on my back that said, "Kiss me" on it. We both had a good laugh and I decided this would be a good time to end the "no fighting lecture."

It is very difficult to get angry with someone who is smiling. Smiling lowers your blood pressure without medication. This seems to be a much cheaper option. Have you ever awakened with a pounding headache on your day off? One of the causes of weekend headaches is a "wrinkled forehead" all week. Muscles have strands of actin and myosin. When muscles flex, actinomycin is formed. The waste product of this is lactic acid. If we form enough lactic acid in our forehead and grind our teeth at night, it is not uncommon to wake up in the morning with a pounding headache behind our eyes in the orbital cavity. One way to reduce this is to smile and laugh on a regular basis. It is virtually impossible to laugh with a wrinkled forehead. I have a simple suggestion for people who fail to laugh every day. Fake it! Do it once, early in the morning if you wish. Get the laugh out of the way early, but do it! I recall being contracted by a local major company that manufactures golf balls. They hired me to work with their employees to help them manage their anger during the summer months. In the various plants, apparently they had a number of confrontations on the line where the employees worked long hours doing repetitive tasks in the hot and humid weather. On the first day of my work, I recall walking towards the front door when a huge voice bellowed, "Hey, where ya going?" It sounded like God! Looking around, I searched for the source of the voice. It was the Pinkerton Guard. She had a huge head. She asked me who my contact person was in the plant. I could not recall the name of the person who hired me. The harder I tried, the more frustrated I felt. The guard said to me, "Well, if you don't come up with a name, you don't get a visitor's pass." I tried as hard as I could, but I could not recall the person who hired me to do the work. I asked the guard, "What is it you want me to do?" The guard said, "Do you have a car?" I responded, "Of course I do!" She responded, "Well, then get in it!" I asked, "What do you want me to do in my car?" She said, "Think of the name. If you think of the name, I'll give you a pass. No name, no pass." I agreed, "Okay." Well, this was not going to be my problem. Remembering my suggestions, I do not want to confront irrational behavior. I am going to keep my sense of humor and I am going to defuse the conflict. So, I said, "Okay, I will get in my car!" She said, "Think of the name." I drove my car to a parking spot, put my seat back, put on a CD, and felt the sun shining through the window onto my face. After a few minutes of this, I felt an emerging shade beginning to cover the car. I opened my eyes and there was the guard. Her head looked like the moon during a solar eclipse. The car cooled from the emerging shade. She yelled, "Open the window!" I looked up and said, "What now?" She responded, "You are now actually straddling two parking places! If you do not move your car, we will not be able to find parking spaces for other people visiting the plant!" That was it! I jumped out of the car and I said, "You know, you don't have to make such a big deal of this! I will...." I turned my head and I saw the person who hired me. I ran over and said, "Kathy, Kathy, she won't let me in the plant! I was here on time! Please let her know I am working to help people manage their anger!" Ironic, isn't it? I wonder who has the anger. Kathy said, "I will take care of it." and she gave me a nametag. It was now time to go into the plant and do my work. But, to do my work, I would have to walk by the Pinkerton Guard. I had two choices. Either walk into the plant and do my job as a professional, or stop and say something. I am not really proud of this. I stopped, looked at the guard and said, "You know, I am so glad that I am not living with you, and you know something, I couldn't imagine you being anyone's mother!" The guard looked at me. I was terrified. The next thing she did, I will never forget. She started to laugh, and laugh and laugh. Tears were rolling down her cheeks, she was laughing so much. She wrapped her massive arms around me and she picked me up and swung me around. She put me down, put her arms in mine and said, "I am yours for the day. Do with me as you please!" I was so surprised. She taught me a lesson I will never forget. There was only one person that day taking himself too seriously, and we all know who he was. She taught me the power of humor; the power of laughter. She was smart enough to defuse my anger by laughing. Ironically enough, they hired me to go into the plant and work with their employees to teach them how to manage their anger, and I am the one who learned a lesson before even walking in the door.

7.   **Do not be intimidated.**

Intimidation is a passive verb. This means nobody can intimidate you unless you allow them to do so. The Pinkerton Guard I met at the front door of the golf ball plant ended up being one of the most charming employees I met that day. She had wonderful dimples when she smiled. However, until she laughed, I let her intimidate me. It is easy to avoid confrontation when you can blame somebody else's behavior for your own avoidance. Intimidation is easy to use as an excuse for passive behavior because it is general enough to use without having to use specific examples. "My boss intimidates me" is a much safer charge than having to specifically address behavior. Therefore, a person's size, job title or reputation can be enough to justify the charge of intimidation. If somebody intimidates you, who has the problem? I suggest that it may be your problem since you are the one allowing yourself to be intimidated.   When dealing with difficult people, it is important to put yourself on the same "playing field" by not allowing yourself to be intimidated. Once you put yourself in a position of being intimidated, you run the risk of exercising non-assertive, passive aggressive, manipulative, avoidance or other forms of dysfunctional communication that deal with difficult people in ways that are self-serving and unproductive.

8.   Avoid defensive behavior.

Do not personalize confrontation.   Once we take a confrontation personally, we begin to add unnecessary energy. Try to depersonalize interactions. People may be disagreeing with what you are thinking and saying, but they are not necessarily angry with you. In Presidential debates, notice how carefully the competing candidates do not respond by personalizing their political positions. "My administration" or "your record suggests" are subtle ways to help the debaters avoid becoming personal. Defensive behavior is very unbecoming. "Are you calling me a liar?" "Are you blaming me?" "That is not my fault." or "I didn't do anything!" tend to project negative energy and risks adding a level of anger that will further alienate the other person. Try not owning the problem. Was I taking the 7th grader wearing a hat in the cafeteria as a challenge to my authority as the Assistant Principal? When I started counting to three, perhaps the hat was becoming less and less the issue. Since it was my job to enforce the school rules, I took the confrontation too personally. Once we personalize conflict, it is a logical step to become defensive. Suddenly compliance becomes less important than winning. Defensive behavior can also become manipulative in nature. For example, when we defensively ask, "Are you blaming me for this problem?" we are fishing for the response, "No, I'm not blaming you!" The "Martyr Syndrome" is a manipulative strategy to enhance our own argument by reducing the personal charge of our adversary. Few strategies can get more in the way of conflict management than defensive behavior. Avoid it at all costs.

9. **Give descriptive, not judgmental, feedback.**

Judgmental feedback risks soliciting defensive responses. Charging someone of abusing sick leave by "calling in sick every Friday" is not as effective as stating, "Are you aware of the fact that you have called in sick 18 out of the last 20 Fridays?" In one instance, we are judging behavior. In the other, we are describing behavior. The more emotionally we deal with difficult people, the more likely we will use judgmental feedback. Descriptive feedback is much easier to hear. Telling a person that he has an "attitude problem" is not particularly useful feedback. Citing specific and recent incidents is not only clearer, it is more useful. Be specific. How helpful is it to use the words always or never? "You never listen to me." "You are always doing things to make people upset." may not be particularly helpful, true or useful. The "manipulative why?" is designed to not manage the conflict, but to simply hurt the other person. For example, how are these "manipulative whys" helpful? "Why are you so stupid?" "Why does nobody like you?" "Why don't you love me the way you used to?" None of these questions are particularly helpful. Describe specific behaviors and avoid the temptations to overstate, judge or exaggerate in an effort to personally diminish the status, dignity and veracity of other people.

Giving descriptive feedback does, of course, take more effort. Insisting that your child "do better" in school is not particularly helpful, unless you describe what "doing better" actually means. Children think in concrete terms. Adults have the capacity to think abstractly. Children think of time in finite terms, while adults think of time in a more infinite context. As a result, parents need to be more descriptive, concrete, and finite in proposing that children "do better" in school. I am a strong advocate of weekly (or perhaps daily if necessary) progress reports for children. While these may be inconvenient for teachers, I found that descriptive and specific feedback like this gives parents a more realistic view of student performance/behavior and a more useful tool for students who require short term, achievable, and immediate feedback. Insisting that your child "stop misbehaving in school" is far less effective than getting a weekly progress report describing specific behaviors and citing more appropriate behaviors demonstrated during the week. Describing a specific incident when a child punched another student in the lunch line is more useful than calling the child a "bully" or guilty of "aggressive behavior." Setting a goal of getting a positive weekly progress report is more meaningful than insisting that the child never touch another child for the rest of his life. In the primary grades, we reward positive behavior by sticking a gold star on the child's forehead. As children get older, we need to be more creative than sticking green Shamrocks on their good papers. What is important here is the need to give feedback. No news is not good news. Everybody requires, indeed craves feedback for effort. Incidentally, even parents, teachers and principals benefit from feedback. Do not tolerate incompetence in our schools. Nobody is more underpaid than a wonderful teacher. On the other hand, there is nobody more overpaid than an incompetent teacher.

10.   **Forgive your parents.**

At first blush, this suggestion may not seem to fit. Ironically, it may be the most important suggestion on my list. Many adults go through life angry at what their parents may or may not have done or said many years ago. This anger or resentment does not go away. Typically, it is buried deeply somewhere. Unfortunately, these feelings are unconsciously the backdrop we use for many of our relationships and interactions. If we do not forgive our parents before they die, we may actually blame them for leaving. If you do not feel comfortable forgiving your parents for them, forgive them for you. This will free you up to go on with your life enjoying healthy productive relationships with others. Be selfish. Forgive them and move on. Guilt is a terrible motivator. Misplacing guilt is not only dysfunctional, it is a hindrance to nurturing healthy relationships. If you choose to hold on to your latent anger towards your parents, you may be surprised at some point to realize that you may be one of the "difficult people" for which lists of suggestions are being generated.

Chapter 20: Leadership is a Performing Art

Anybody can be a leader. You do not have to be smart, right or even nice to be a leader. There is only one thing that leaders require. They need a follower. If you turn around and you see somebody following you, then you are a leader. It is easy to be a boss. God makes bosses. If there is a vacancy, you send in your resume, you pray to God, and you go to an interview. God looks down upon you and announces, "Thou art the boss." Bosses are not always leaders. There are lots of people in the workplace who are bosses, but not leaders. Conversely, there are lots of leaders who are not bosses. I always felt some of the strongest leaders in our schools were not even adults. Watch first grade children on the playground, and you will see strong leaders. Certain 6-year-olds run around during recess and a clump of their classmates follow. These little 6-year-old leaders never took a class on leadership and they have no idea what "quadrant of leadership styles" they fall into. While management is a science, leadership is a performing art.

There are differences between clumps and teams. Clumps are made up of people who are together, but not working together on a common task. Eleven people on a field are not a football team unless they are playing football. Clumps are people with nothing to do. Teams are clumps with tasks. Leaders always emerge from teams. Leaders in the workplace who consistently get turned down for job promotions leading to management positions often become active union leaders. They use their leadership skills in ways that provide for them a sense of appreciation and recognition. I think we tend to over think the notion of leadership. If groups of people need somebody to meet their immediate needs, they seek, identify, and appoint a leader. The "appointment" is informal, but every bit as powerful as any corporate promotion. Because groups often have changing needs, the notion of leadership can be quite fluid. During times of transition and change, leaders readily emerge. Often times they fill a void caused by a manager fearful to provide direction. During uncertain times, leaders are often the sole source of information for employees. This information is often times characterized as rumor. Nature abhors a vacuum. The workplace is no different in this regard. In the absence of information, leaders emerge meeting the need for information and communication. The information may or may not be accurate, but no news is often worse than bad news. People often seek information, even if they suspect its veracity. Do you really think that readers believe every word written in a tabloid?

While all human beings are different, I am convinced that we can generally predict behavior. The science of predicting behavior is called management. I am also certain that we can treat individuals differently and be perfectly consistent doing it. First, let's explore the notion that human behavior can generally be predicted. Try this exercise.

1. Think of a number between 1 and 9

2. Take that number and multiply it times 9.

3. You now have a two digit number. Add the two digits. Subtract 5 from that number.

4. You now have a smaller single digit number. We are now going to change that number into a letter. Here is how:

5. If it is 1, make it an A. If it is 2, make it a B. If it is 3, make it a C. If it is 4, make it a D. If it is 5, make it an E. If it is 6, make it an F. (Using this formula, change your digit into a letter).

6. Think of a country that starts with your new letter.

7. Look at the second letter in the country that you just picked.

8. Think of an animal that starts with that letter.

9. Think of the color of the animal that you picked.

Did you end up with the color gray? If you are like 98% of the population, you did. After all, that is the color of an elephant that came from Denmark. Is it not?

Next, let us explore the apparent paradox of treating people differently and being perfectly consistent doing so. If you have more than one child, ask yourself two questions. Are they different? My guess is that you said yes to this one. My three sons may have the same color hair and eyes, but their personalities could not be any more different. One would do his homework without being told, one would simply ignore the homework assignment, and the other one would do the assignment, lose it and then blame everybody else for moving it. My oldest son is nearly compulsive, in terms of how neatly he keeps his things. My youngest son's bedroom was so unbelievably disastrous that it would take an archeological dig to find the carpet! Yes, our kids can be quite different from each other even with the exact same genetic makeup. Now that we have determined how different our children are, did we treat them differently? I suggest again, yes we did. Some kids need to have their hand held to get them to do anything. Other kids need for us to get out of their way and let them go. People in management call this "maturity;" not in the sense of age, but in terms of how "self-directive" we are. People who require little structure are said to be mature, while those who need lots of structure and direction are said to be immature. Corporations, companies, teams and even families have members who represent both maturity extremes. Therefore, we need to provide the kind of structure that is consistent with the person's maturity level. Hence, we consistently apply this criteria as we treat people differently.

When I was an elementary school principal, I soon learned that the biggest decision that could ever be made in a school is the issue of indoor or outdoor recess. Everybody dreaded indoor recess. Try supervising a class of 7-year-olds inside and you will soon appreciate why we avoided indoor recesses whenever we could. Every September, I began the new school year with my opening faculty meeting. I would then list a series of announcements. One agenda item each year was my annual indoor/outdoor recess announcement. It read something like this: "Teachers, regarding recess this year, if it is raining outside, it is indoor recess. If it is not raining outside and suitable for children to go outside, it is outdoor recess. The person making this decision will be the teacher who has recess duty that day." Sounds simple enough, does it not? This should work for the teachers, right? I figured that I would leave this decision in the hands of the teachers for matters regarding drizzle, puddles and other variances of the "rain theme."

One day, it was raining so hard that you could not see the tops of the trees. The rain was pouring sideways. The wind was howling and lakes were beginning to form on the asphalt driveway. Little rivers were pouring into the roadside drains. As I walked through the building, I spotted outside what was certain to be a mirage. I actually spotted one of my teachers outside hunched over in a fetal position, water pelting the back of her raincoat, and hair hanging straight down the sides of her face with streams of water dripping off the ends of her hair forming a puddle under her face. I could not believe my eyes! In front of her were 40-50 second graders gleefully running around the hot top area playing a game of who could make the biggest splash with their shoes. Horrified, I opened the outside door and used my "Mr. Bossio voice" to get everyone inside. Apparently, this teacher is going to require a tad more supervision in regard to the recess "go or no go decision." The next time it was her turn for recess duty, can you guess who made the decision? Obviously, I had her check with me. When she began to sense a pattern beginning to emerge, I weaned her off me. Everybody has a gift. Our job is to find that gift in ourselves and others. Apparently this teacher's gift was not good judgment. In all other ways, she was a wonderful teacher. I just had to be more aware of the recess duty schedule, particularly when it was cloudy outside and her day to decide.

I once had a school head custodian named Franklin. He was absolutely wonderful. Although he was nearing retirement age, Frank was devoted to the school and dedicated to doing everything he could to make the facility clean and ready for all the children and staff. He was extremely conscientious. Franklin was a perfectionist in a job where perfection and thoroughness were essential. Everybody loved him. He was warm, friendly and open to anything that anybody ever asked him to do. In many ways, he was the perfect head custodian. My experience with custodians in my schools was not very good. I have had custodians who have slept under the stairwell at night, stolen teachers' lunches out of the refrigerator, drank alcohol on the job, and even admitted to indecent exposure to one of my teachers during off school hours. Clearly, Franklin was every principal's dream. He had one problem. He was very reluctant to take any initiative. He was so afraid of making a mistake that he would wait to be told to do things, as opposed to seeing a problem, taking some initiative and fixing it. Like many of us, he sought and he craved approval. He worked at the school for virtually more years than I was alive. He was adored throughout the entire community for his lifelong commitment to the school.

One day, Franklin knocked on my door stating that there was some sort of emergency. When I asked him to come in, he was obviously flustered. He stated that the heating units in pod 3 were not working. He further stated that the kids and teachers were freezing, that they were wearing their coats, and you could see their breaths as they spoke. He said the temperature outside was 7 degrees Fahrenheit and if something was not done immediately, he feared the pipes would freeze. He asked, "Mr. Bossio, what do you want me to do?" Bewildered, I retorted, "Franklin, go fix them." Impressed apparently with my simple, yet elegant management style, Franklin responded with the awe of a child sitting on the lap of Santa Claus by saying, "Good idea Mr. Bossio!" and off he went. Approximately an hour later, Franklin returned to my office with a less urgent, but equally animated announcement as he stuck his head into my office with the pronouncement, "I fixed them." I responded with a wry smile and an appreciative, "Well done Frank! Thank you so much!" It occurred to me that if I were such an effective leader, perhaps I should have empowered Franklin to make these kinds of decisions without my direction. Sometimes we actually enjoy the "need to be needed." Have you ever heard anybody say that they do not want you to do anything until you check with them? This kind of dependency is not organizationally healthy. This is not leadership, it is dependency. Can you imagine if I were not in the building when Franklin realized that the heating units were not working? Would he in fact have let the pipes freeze as opposed to fixing them without my sanction? It appears to me that we need to empower children and adults to take the necessary risks to act independently. People will only do so when they feel safe. There is no quicker way to discourage self-direction, initiative and risk taking than to second guess people. Leadership is like parenting in many ways. We parent our children with the hopes that some day they will not need us. Strong leaders seek to build systems of people who can work independently, yet collaboratively. I suspect that some bosses may fear this kind of self-direction and independence. After all, if the goal of a boss is to develop a staff of subordinates who do not need him, what happens to the boss when the company is going through a period of downsizing or management staff reductions? This may be the ultimate catch-22 for the leader truly dedicated to employee empowerment. It is always nice to be needed, but building this kind of dependence is counterproductive in the workplace and downright inconvenient at home. At 18, they will come back. At 21, they will come back and they bring people with them.

Franklin retired and he was replaced by his assistant, Richard. Richard learned well from Franklin. One afternoon, Richard came running into my office with an urgent tone in his voice, "Mr. Bossio, come with me! You have to see this!" Having learned my lesson with Franklin, I calmly responded, "Richard, is this an emergency and something I really need to see or is this something that you can take care of?" Richard assured me that this was something I would really need to see in person. After walking through what seemed like the entire building, Richard stopped at the boys' room, opened the door and invited me in. Reluctantly, but curiously, I entered the boys' room with Richard. However, Richard was not finished with the tour. He walked over to the stall, opened the door and again invited me in. Now, I have a decision to make. Am I going into this stall with Richard without knowing why? Well, I have come this far, why not? He assured me that this was important. As we entered the stall, the door shut behind us. I recall praying to God that no child walked into the boys' room and noticed Mr. Bossio and Richard in the stall with the door shut. As we walked over to the water closet, we both stood across from each other forehead to forehead looking down into the water. Apparently, some kid had clogged up the toilet with a towel of some sort, flushed the toilet, and then threw in several blackboard erasers into the almost overflowing water. I recall that it looked like little black felt boats racing counterclockwise in a mini ceramic version of an Olympic pool. Part of me was relieved and part of me was frustrated. I simply looked at Richard and told him, "Please unclog the toilet." With all the reverence of my authority that he could muster and with the dutiful diligence and subordination he learned from Franklin, Richard dove into the toilet with water up to his armpits to fix the problem. I walked back to my office disappointed with myself for not having learned my lesson from Franklin. Leaders teach others to act in ways that fulfill needs. If a need emerges, teams look for a leader to meet that need. The best leaders do not tell people what to do, but rather they show them what to do. In a perverse, but humbling thought, it occurred to me that Franklin may have been a more effective leader than I. Our children learn to parent by modeling our behavior. Richard learned how to act by watching Franklin. As parents, perhaps we need to be cognizant of what we are teaching our children. As the school principal, I learned to adjust my management style in such a way so as to empower others to take care of routine matters and to reserve "checking with me" for more important issues.

In this way, we will hopefully allow our children to feel more confident, secure and free to take measured risks and, as a result, grow up to be self-directive, independent and mature adults. Clearly children are not the only people who learn in our schools.

Mother Theresa wrote a wonderful narrative about doing good. I have taken out her religious references to make her words more secular and more applicable to leadership. Her words talk about serving others and I cannot think of a better way to end this chapter.

People are unreasonable, illogical and self-centered.

Love them anyway.

If you do good, people accuse you of selfish ulterior motives.

Do good anyway.

If you are successful, you will win false friends and true enemies.

Succeed anyway.

Honesty and frankness will make you vulnerable.

Be honest and frank anyway.

The good you do today will be forgotten tomorrow.

Do good anyway.

The biggest people with the biggest ideas can be shot down by
the smallest   people with the smallest minds.

Think big anyway.

People favor underdogs, but always follow top dogs.

Fight for some underdogs anyway.

What you spend years building may be destroyed overnight.

Build it anyway.

Give the world the best you've got, and you might get kicked
in the teeth.

Give the world the best you've got anyway.

Chapter 21: Free Crab Rangoons

Have you ever caught yourself underestimating yourself or others? When we underestimate human capacities and abilities, we shortchange potential. Few endeavors are more harmful to becoming self-actualized than to underestimate our own ability to prevail over life's difficulties. When we underestimate others, we deny them opportunities. At best, this can be unfair. At worst, it can be discriminatory. Be careful. There are laws protecting people from this kind of arbitrary, preconceived and insidious notion of potential. Few people would openly describe themselves as biased or discriminatory in how they view others. The legal doctrine of "reasonable accommodation" in the workplace is based on the notion that it is the employer's responsibility to adjust conditions to maximize employee performance, despite an apparent "disability." Occasionally, however, even the most well meaning and enlightened person will behave in a manner that belies deep-seated presumptions about a person's abilities, or more to the point, disabilities. Life has enough icebergs without contriving them.

It was an early Friday evening and I had just returned from an extended out-of-state speaking engagement. I was tired, glad to be home and starved. I was struggling with conflicting physiological needs. I was so tired that part of me just wanted to settle in, go to bed early and catch up on my rest. The other part of me was so famished that I wanted to eat anything I could get my hands on. Was I going to bed early or was I going to eat? My empty belly settled the question. No longer ambivalent, I headed out to a nearby Chinese restaurant to order takeout. The plan was clear. I was going to order a Pu-Pu Platter for two and an order of Subgum Chicken fried rice. I was then going to go home, sit in my bed like the Buddha in front of the television and satiate myself with a bottle of Diet Ginger Ale until I could no longer engorge myself or no longer stay awake, whichever came first.

After entering the restaurant, I eagerly approached the lobby counter to order my dinner. With the eagerness of a child enumerating his Christmas list for Santa, I described my order. After paying the bill, I was told that it would take awhile for my order to be ready, and that perhaps I could sit in the lounge area and wait there for my takeout order. The associate said that he would bring the bagged order to me when it was ready. Immediately, I entered the crowded lounge, found a few empty seats at the bar, bellied up to the bar, ordered a small Scorpion Bowl and listened to the Karaoke. I am very reluctant to criticize Karaoke singers because they could not make enough Scorpion Bowls for me to ever get up in front of another human being, let alone a lounge full of strangers, and attempt to sing from a screen of moving lyrics. There is a quantum difference between speaking and singing in front of an audience. Thankfully, I know the difference.

Soon after I settled in, I noticed a woman with a white walking cane enter the lounge. Beside her was a woman skillfully guiding her through the maze of lounge patrons. It was apparent that the woman with the white cane was blind. The two women navigated their way to the empty seats beside me at the bar. I watched as inconspicuously as possible as the blind woman folded up her white cane and settled in next to me. I overheard the two women talking. Apparently, it was the blind woman's birthday and her caretaker was taking her out for a couple of birthday drinks. Of course, I wished the blind woman a happy birthday and I offered to buy her a drink. She accepted my offer and we started a very pleasant, but benign conversation. Moments after we started chatting, the caretaker said that she was going outside for a cigarette. She asked me if I would save her seat, watch her pocketbook and keep an eye on her friend. Of course, I gratuitously said that I would be happy to help her in any way that I could while she was outside. As soon as the caretaker left, three huge open containers of Chinese food were placed in front of the blind woman. Apparently they had already ordered the food and the two of them were going to dine at the bar. I cannot begin to describe how good the food looked and smelled. The three stainless steel containers were stuffed with crab rangoons, chicken wings, spare ribs, egg rolls, chicken teriyaki, pork strips and other   unidentifiable, but equally appealing appetizers. My stomach was growling, my mouth was salivating and I could not take my eyes off of the way the lounge lights glistened off the steamy array of inviting Chinese tidbits. Now, let me set the scene. Here I sit, waiting for my takeout order to arrive and I am starving to death. Next to me is a blind woman with three open containers of delectable appetizers in front of her. And to top it all off, her caretaker was outside smoking a cigarette. Do you see where this is going? Please understand, I am not proud of this.

After scanning the lounge for any potential eye witnesses, I noted a crab rangoon begging me to taste it. We are all familiar with the notion of how quickly Chinese food can spoil when left unattended in an unprotected open environment. Food poisoning can be very painful and potentially fatal. It is my duty to protect this vulnerable blind woman sitting in the middle of the hostile environment of the Karaoke lounge. Succumbing to the temptation, I casually reached for the "forbidden fruit." Now, please remember that I am starving to death, I bought the blind woman a drink and I am saving her friend's seat.   How much could a blind woman miss one appetizer? I suppose this is a feeble and transparent attempt to rationalize my behavior.   I gummed the crab rangoon as quietly as I could. As I became more and more brazen, one could probably imagine that the initial crab rangoon led to a chicken wing, then to a sparerib, and finally to any appetizer that was within my reach. The blind woman's food was fast becoming my unexpected buffet. After several minutes of this carnage, a pile of bones was beginning to form under my chin. The evidence was obvious. I am stealing food from a blind person.

All good things must come to an end. As you can see, I am using the term "good" loosely here. As I noticed the caretaker re-entering the lounge, it was obvious that the buffet was over. Quickly, I discarded the evidence. I wiped my greasy lips with a napkin and like a hawk, I swooped down upon the emerging pile of bones. With one skillful motion, I swiped the bones to the floor. I am not sure if I felt guilty at this point, but I do know that I was not starving anymore. Perhaps I will face my punishment on judgment day when I pass on to the great Chinese restaurant in the sky. No, God was not going to wait to reconcile my misdeed. Justice can sometimes be swift and without mercy. As the returning caretaker approached her seat, I nodded my head and smiled as if to say that everything was fine. However, my new blind friend had a very different perspective. She immediately turned and blurted out to the caretaker, "Thank God you're back! This guy has been stealing all my damn food!" I wanted to die. I wanted the earth to open up and swallow me whole. What could I say? Did she see me eating her food? Could she hear my chewing? Did she see shadows of my hand passing back and forth in front of her? Did she sense a gentle breeze stirred by the motion of my arm? It did not matter how she knew. The fact is that she was aware of my indiscretion. My lesson here is simple. Never underestimate human potential and abilities.

Chapter 22: Do Not Laugh at Mysteries

Mom has a habit of making crisis calls. She is understandably lonely since she lives alone and she is suffering from the debilitating symptoms of Parkinson's disease. As a result, it is not uncommon for her to call me with a problem that requires an immediate visit. Whether it be a bad dream, a stuck garage door, lost glasses, something stuck in her tooth, a ride to the dentist to get her teeth cleaned, 3 AM hallucinations, a broken telephone (As of this moment, I have purchased 6 telephones for her), a computer problem (She forgot her password), a dead mouse on the walkway, prescription shoes that must be returned immediately because they do not have Velcro and she is on the 14th day of an alleged 15 day return policy window, or a myriad of other issues that require immediate attention, it is not unusual to receive a crisis call from Mom. Generally between Brian and me, we are able to drive to Braintree to fix the problem. So, when I received a call to take her to Milton Hospital in Milton, MA, I was not surprised. She did not want to go to Milton Hospital for any particular medical problem. We generally use the emergency room at South Shore Hospital in Weymouth for her medical emergencies. This request was different.

Apparently, one of the windows at Milton Hospital had an apparition of the Virgin Mary holding Baby Jesus. The window was receiving a great deal of local and national attention as hordes of people were visiting the hospital to view this window. National networks, Fox News, CNN and virtually every news outlet was covering the miracle of the Virgin Mary's appearance at Milton Hospital. Mom called me because she wanted to see the window. She wanted me to take her to view Mary. My first reaction was to try to discourage her. I lectured Mom that when Thermopane window seals are broken, the gas escapes and the cloud of moisture that forms between the layers of glass often takes the form of various images. With a good imagination, you can see anything you want in puffy clouds, plaster patterns on ceilings or, of course, in hospital windows. I told her that I had a lot of things to do on my day off and that I would not be available to take her to see the window. Mom gracefully said that she understood and that it was okay. We said goodbye and we hung up the phone. Immediately, I felt terribly guilty. I could not shake the tremendous sense of letting my Mom down. Think of what happened. My widowed Mom, dying of Parkinson's disease, asked her only child on his day off to take her to see the Virgin Mary at a hospital that was less than 15 miles from her house. People were literally traveling from all over the world to see the window, and I said no. Frankly, I felt like a real jerk. I immediately called my Mom, told her to get dressed and I informed her that I was on my way to pick her up so we could check out the window ourselves.

The drive to Milton Hospital was complicated only by my Mom's insistence that she knew exactly how to get there. Since my Mom is the only person in the world who may be as stubborn as I am, she convinced me to trust her directions. About an hour later, it was obvious that she had no idea how to get there. I figured that this was fate's way of slapping me on the wrist for initially saying no to Mom. Eventually, we found the entrance to Milton Hospital. I was surprised to see so many cars approaching the hospital entrance. In fact, there was a man directing the traffic toward a specific parking lot with an arrow and a sign identifying the lot as the "Window Viewing Parking Area." After parking the car and lots of "eye-rolling," I helped Mom into her wheelchair, locked the car and headed up the hill to see the throng of "true believers." I must admit that I was quite curious to see the hospital window that had drawn so much worldwide attention. Typically, I am skeptical about claims related to alleged religious images in cheeseburgers, clouds, Frito Lay potato chips, grilled cheese sandwiches, Thermopane windows and various other art mediums. I believe that sometimes we see what we hope to see. I do admit to straddling the line between fascination and skepticism when it comes to a natural phenomenon. I was, however, crushed when I heard that New Hampshire's Old Man in the Mountain had lost his facial features to time and erosion. The logical, rational, left-brain part of me tempered my interest in this little driving adventure to the hospital. On the other hand, my curiosity, childlike enthusiasm, and passion for exploring life's mysteries put a little dance to my step as I pushed Mom in her wheelchair.

Feeling playful, I came up with an idea. Mom has a good sense of humor and I am sure that she will go along with my plan. I asked Mom, "Hey, do you want to be on the 6 o'clock news with me tonight?" Mom responded with a wry smile, "Sure. What do you have in mind?" I told Mom that I would roll the wheelchair right up to and in front of the hospital window with the Virgin Mary image on it. When I give the cue, I want her to jump out of the wheelchair and start bouncing up and down and yell as loudly as she can, "It's a miracle! I can walk again. It's a miracle!" I will then join her unbridled celebration and we will surely be noticed as newsworthy by the many television networks covering the hospital window attraction. Mom thought it would be fun and she agreed with the sacrilegious plan.

We approached the hospital building. Several hundred onlookers were solemnly looking up at the window. Priests, nuns, families and children with impairments were kneeling before the window. Candles were lit, and pictures of presumably deceased loved ones with flowers were leaning against the building foundation. A murmur of prayer could be heard throughout the general area of viewing. The atmosphere was far more solemn than I expected. Somehow, I assumed that the setting would be more casual and festive. Mom and I looked up at the window. Neither one of us uttered a single word. I put my hand on my Mom's shoulders and I said sternly and deliberately, "Don't you dare get out of that wheelchair." I promised that if she stood up, I would pretend to be a perfect stranger. Both of us were stunned with the inexplicable details of the image. For a Thermopane window with a broken seal, the detail of Mary's features and robe, and even the face of Baby Jesus were a bit more impressive than we had expected. We were humbled into spontaneously canceling our mock celebration. This was not a carnival. Whatever we were looking at inspired tremendous faith among the many believers surrounding us. We stood quietly in our own thoughts for about 20 minutes. Without a word, I turned Mom's wheelchair around and we returned back to the car with a mixture of feelings ranging from embarrassment to humility and reverence. The universe is filled with mysteries. I have no idea what Mom and I looked at that day. I am a firm believer that we should never lose our sense of humor and that laughter is a tremendous coping mechanism for life's daily challenges. However, I also believe that we should not laugh at mysteries we do not understand. I have a feeling that God may have a sense of humor.

I ran across a brief narrative written by an unknown author that touches my belief system in ways that inspire me. Edited to suit my own purposes, the narrative follows:

I believe that imagination is stronger than knowledge...
...that myth is more potent than history.

I believe that dreams are more powerful than facts...
...that hope always triumphs over experience...
...that laughter is the only cure for sadness.

I believe that love is stronger than grief.

Chapter 23: Watch Out for Icebergs!

Everyone has icebergs in their lives. Some of the icebergs hide under the surface and sneak up on us, while others are more obvious and lie directly in front of us. Life is neither fair nor easy. Whether it be my Dad's passing, my Mom's Parkinson's, my divorce, the failure of Jeffrey's first marriage, Karen's first pregnancy ending in the first term when the fetus' heart stopped, or Mrs. Gutterson telling my Mom that I am not college material, we face icebergs on a regular basis. We make mistakes. We take risks every day. We can devote our energies trying to avoid mistakes by not taking risks. An argument can be made that playing it safe and taking no risks may be one of life's biggest mistakes. Change, opportunity, and growth all require taking chances. Part of being an entrepreneur is to take measured risks. We learn from failure. We learn not to pursue courses of action that provide pain, frustration and other negative consequences. Even a child will not touch a hot oven twice! One definition of insanity is doing the same things over and over again and expecting different results.

I gave up a wonderful job as school superintendent to start a new business. I was well paid and I loved my superintendency. I worked in an affluent supportive community with extraordinary children and a highly motivated and professional staff. I received a fine paycheck every two weeks, enjoyed a great health plan, was in line to receive a good pension, enjoyed tremendous working conditions, and generally could not ask for more job satisfaction. However, I had been public speaking as a hobby for almost ten years. I absolutely loved it. For the first several years, I spoke for no fees. When I started getting paid, I could not believe that I could be paid for having so much fun. In one year, I made more money public speaking than I received as a school superintendent. When life gives you choices, go with your heart. I resigned from my superintendency, gave up all the security and benefits, and took the leap of faith. The local newspaper, The Beacon, cited my comment as the quote of the week; "It will be unusual in the fact that I probably won't be back working in a public school in the foreseeable future, but it is also exciting in that I now have the chance to experience the risks and potential that only a new adventure can bring."

I am very proud of my business. My middle son, Brian, works for me full-time and we have an excellent record of seamless service to our customers. Brian does a wonderful job ironing out all the details necessary to assure that I am prepared and show up at the right place, on time, and ready to speak. Because we do so many speaking engagements, it is easy to appreciate how important it is to make certain that all details are covered. Our record of success in this regard speaks for itself. However, there are icebergs that appear on occasion. The following jobs did not quite work out as well as they were planned:

1. I was once let off at 2:00 a.m. by my limousine driver at the wrong conference center in upstate Arkansas for a keynote speech I was about to give at 9:00 a.m. at a conference center two hours away.

2. One cold evening, I stood outside at Atlanta, GA Airport waiting for my ride to take me to a hotel to give an 8:30 a.m. keynote address to a national newspaper group. Unfortunately, my ride never came and none of my paperwork said where the conference was going to be held.

3. Several years ago, I rushed into a convention hall where several conferences were being held. I was about 15 minutes early for my after dinner speech. I rushed in , sat down, chatted briefly with the folks at the table and waited for my introduction. As I sat there, listening to the introduction, I was mortified to hear that I was not the one

being introduced. I was at the wrong conference. I was to speak at the one in the next room.

4. I once appeared at a conference in downtown Springfield for a job that was scheduled over a year earlier. Unfortunately, the person who hired me had left that job and failed to tell anybody that he had hired me to speak at the conference. I was so embarrassed standing there insisting I was their speaker right in front of the other fellow, who insisted that he was their speaker.

5. Phoenix, AZ, I was the opening speaker at a Johnson & Johnson National Sales Meeting. After a very impressive introduction and a beautiful light show, I spoke to the 500 attendees with my zipper at low mast. I was wondering why the first two rows thought my material was so funny.

6. Brian paged me just before I was to give a 9:00 a.m. speech in Washington, DC. He reluctantly informed me that my 8:00 p.m. speech that evening at the Seekonk Chamber of Commerce was actually an 8:00 a.m. breakfast speech and that 200 people were sitting at a Seekonk, MA restaurant waiting for me. Brian wanted to know what he should tell them.

7. We once had a group in New York insist that they had me booked for a speaking engagement. Brian recalls speaking to them about open dates, but nothing for sure had been

scheduled. Large audiences of people waiting for me to show up at a job that I knew nothing about does little to enhance our professional reputation.

8. I missed a speaking engagement in Bethel, ME once because I set the alarm for 4:00 p.m. instead of 4:00 a.m. I woke up in terror to see the clock showing 9:00 a.m. when I was supposed to be on my feet at a conference at the Bethel Inn, a four hour drive. Brian is very conscientious when he schedules, negotiates and works with our large customer base. However, with such a volume of work, mix-ups are bound to occur. Just for the record, however, any job that I ever missed was rescheduled and I spoke without charge to the customer. Our reputation for quality and reliable service is a trademark of my business. However, to quote the popular radio syndicated personality, Paul Harvey, "Now you know the rest of the story."

Being an elementary school principal also has its share of crises. I recall receiving a handwritten note from a parent asking if her second grader could bring a pet duck to school for class show and tell. Since I was busy attending to "more important" matters, I literally dismissed the note as frivolous and I assumed that the parent would understand my tacit approval by virtue of the fact that I did not deny her written request. After all, good time management suggests to busy administrators that they not bog down in routine matters and to utilize the valuable resource of time by attending to more important tasks. It is insinuated that many managers procrastinate doing unpleasant tasks by staying busy doing more fun activities. It was always easy for me to find lots of things to do in a school, rather than shut the door and focus on teacher evaluations, budgets and other more mundane, but nevertheless, important administrative tasks. In any case, I have many more important issues to address than the question of a child bringing a duck to school. Do you recognize foreshadowing?

Several weeks passed. One early morning after all the buses had arrived, my secretary came running into my office. She was highly animated as she announced that there was some sort of emergency in the second grade wing. As I left my office, I took off my suit jacket. Good crisis managers always do this before attending to any emergency. When I entered the general office area, I could hear over the intercom speaker a commotion coming from one of the second grade classes. I heard a combination of children screaming, furniture being tossed around, adult shrieking, lots of laughing, and as you probably have already guessed, the sound of a duck quacking. I ran down the corridor as fast as I could, being closely followed by my secretary, the custodian and any other adult close enough to see the calamity escalate. It is ironic that the principal would run down the corridor since the school rule strictly prohibits running in the hallways. The visual reminded me of the old "Mighty Mouse" cartoons with the song, "Here he comes to save the day" which always accompanied the hero when he flew to fix the crisis at hand. As I passed classrooms, teachers and children stretched their necks out the door to see why Mr. Bossio was breaking his own school rule. I finally reached the classroom. I will never forget the visual that faced me when I entered the room. The teacher was huddled in the corner. I am not sure if she was laughing or crying. Chairs and desks were strewn all over the floor. Twenty-two children were chasing the most massive white duck I had ever seen in my life. Its legs had to be two feet long. Its webbed feet looked like swim flippers, and its bill was the size of a catcher's mitt. There was duck dung all over the floor and unfortunately it was all over the children's clothes. Like any good crisis manager, I took charge. I yelled out in vintage "Mr. Bossio" voice, "Freeze!" Every child froze in his tracks. I even think the duck was startled enough to stop quacking for the moment. I then ordered all the children to line up against the wall.

Immediately, every child complied. Each child was standing in a straight line against the wall. The teacher began to stand up straight in the corner to observe the master take charge of the runaway duck crisis. The doorway was swelling with assorted observers of what was to become a classic principal/duck confrontation. Can you guess what happened next? I chased the duck. I scrambled over the desks and chairs. I slipped on the floor slick with duck dung. I grabbed the duck by its massive butt. Its tail feathers flicked my fresh white shirt and stained my tie. Finally, I caught the quacking water fowl villain. I felt so proud to be able to catch the duck when 22 children had failed. I walked over to the teacher and asked her where she would like me to put the duck. Out of a sense of propriety and good taste, I will not repeat where she told me to stick it. The teacher pointed to a peach basket. Now remember, this duck's legs were nearly two feet long, and the peach basket was no more than one foot deep. There was no way that the peach basket was going to be able to contain this quacking rebel. I asked my secretary to call the mother so she could come to the school to pick up this duck. As I returned to my office, hoards of children and adults lined the hallways and applauded my heroic efforts. Nevertheless, I learned a number of valuable lessons from this incident.

1. Be careful what "routine matters" we ignore in favor of more "important issues." This incident could have been tragic. Imagine if this incident occurred on a school bus.

2. Unfortunately, crisis management feels wonderful. Despite my stupidity, I was applauded for "saving the day." If I were so smart, I would have answered the initial letter and I would have made certain that the duck would be transported in a secure and appropriate cage.

3. Crisis management looks good. When people re-told the story, they described me in complimentary terms.

4. Always keep a spare white shirt and an extra tie in your office.

Chapter 24: Updates

Much has happened since I starting writing this book. As in any slice of life, new and exciting events and occasional icebergs appear. Let me update you on a number of matters related to my journey.

Each year during a winter lull in my travel schedule, Brian schedules an annual trip to Disney World. From February 6th through February 14th of 2005, we stayed at the Disney Boardwalk. Imagine watching the Patriots defeating the Eagles in the Super Bowl with two angels sitting on Grampa's lap sharing a massive bucket of chicken wings. I thought I had died and gone to heaven. Colin loved the game room, Makayla loved feeding the ducks, Karen loved the stores and Brian loved the fact that Grampa was paying for the trip. As usual, I was available to babysit every night as Brian and Karen hit the hot spots in Pleasure Island. This year, however, they pooped out and spent most of the nights crashed in the hotel room from all of the walking during the day. Colin took his first ride on Space Mountain. He was 45" tall this year. Makayla met EVERY princess in the Magic Kingdom. I think I spent about $200.00 in quarters in the game room with the kids. However, it was worth it because Colin won an Elmo in the grab game.

He generously gave it to Makayla. She batted her eyes at her hero. Each morning, Colin and I sneaked out to the game room and we fed the ducks before Makayla woke up and figured out that Colin and Grampa were missing. As long as we returned quickly to the room with coffee for Daddy, Diet Coke for Mommy, and a frosted doughnut for Makayla, all was forgiven. Each night we returned to our room with several new stuffed animals. You can imagine what the room looked like by the end of the week. Proudly, the kids would line them up and review exactly how they won them. In one case, we manipulated one game so that ONLY Colin and Makayla were competing for the stuffed prize. It is amazing how Makayla held her own against all competition. I so love spending time with those two kids. Disney is a special place. Only there would grownups walk around in mouse ears. Think about it. Three-dollars and fifty cents for bottled water, $45.00 for a Mickey sweatshirt (multiplied times five), $8.25 for a tube of tan lotion, $4,800.00 for the room, $2.50 for a small coffee, $200.00 for crystal pictures of the kids, $1,000.00 for a van rental, $27.00 for a princess crown, $4.00 per Disney pin, $63.00 for a fast pass, $27.00 for a Space Mountain shirt, $4.50 for a box of popcorn, $5.00 per valet, per parking and per retrieval, several hundred dollars per week for five day passes, $3.75 for a bagel, $45.00 per lunch, $126.00 per dinner, 3.50 per Mickey

Mouse ice cream sandwich and $200.00 for an Elmo. Now I know what they mean by "Disney Magic," and I have learned that it is worth every penny.

On May 2, 2005, my oldest son, Jeffrey's wife, Jill, gave birth to a gorgeous 7 lb. 10 oz baby boy named Noah Thomas. Several months later, they announced that Jill was pregnant again. Not to be outdone, Brian's wife, Karen, gave Colin and Makayla a new brother on July 21, 2005, 7 lb. 6 oz. Tyler Norman. Yes, they named the baby after me. It was such a simple, yet elegant gift. I purchased a Howard Miller grandfather's clock with four little plaques on it engraved with the names of Colin Christopher, Makayla Ashley, Noah Thomas and Tyler Norman, and their birth dates. I figured I would get Tyler's name engraved with my name before Karen and Brian changed their minds.

On November 8, 2005, I had surgery for an inguinal hernia. Apparently, I inherited the inguinal weakness from my Dad. The hernia appeared the morning before I gave six one-hour presentations at a major medical center in the State of Washington. You can only imagine how uncomfortable I was giving six speeches in one day to hundreds of doctors, nurses and other hospital support staff with my lower intestines bulging through my upper groin area. I was determined to perform without my audience suspecting that I was in excruciating pain. When I called Brian during one of the breaks to make an appointment with my primary care physician for a referral to a surgeon, Brian suggested that I just go to the lavatory, drop my trousers, show one of the doctors my groin area and stay at the hospital and get it fixed. I suggested to Brian that surgery may be a bit more complicated than that. After my successful surgery on November 18th, I had 12 days to get ready for four out-of-state speaking engagements on December 1st and 2nd. My surgeon prescribed Vicodin for pain; however, I only wanted to use Advil. My surgeon suggested that I not return to work for three weeks and that when I do, I should be sitting down for my speeches. Apparently my surgeon did not study type A behavior in medical school. On the third day after my surgery, I was walking one mile. On day 5, I was walking four miles. By the time December 1st had arrived, I was 100% recovered and ready to work and travel full-time. I now walk four miles virtually every day. The type A part of me wants to walk every day, rain or shine. The type B side of me is less compulsive and might defer a day's walk if the weather is inclement. The left brain part of me has already computed that a four mile walk at 4 mph pace, at 150 lbs., for a duration of 65 minutes will burn 488 calories. The right brain side of me is considering another route that has more interesting scenery than the boring industrial park that I have been using. The perfectionist in me is challenged when I view a misspelled sign in the driveway of the distribution center I use to mark the halfway point of my daily walk. The sign reads "Recieving."

Jeffrey has quit his job to work fewer hours, to be able to stay home with Noah. His wife, Jill, works as a nurse practitioner. They are working hard at balancing the ongoing demands of work, childcare and parenting. Andrew has gone back to school to become a registered nurse. Andy has faced a few icebergs in his life. The most current one is an apparent delay before he can begin his nursing classes. I am certain that it will work out. He already has degrees in auto body and exercise physiology. Vikki works in a special needs residential facility. Mom is doing reasonably well with her Parkinson's. She no longer drives, but she is willing to go to family events as long as I drive her and I promise not to dress her up as a witch.

Brian recently had the chance of a lifetime. His name was drawn in a contest sponsored by Mohegan Sun to shoot a 3-point basketball shot for $7,770.00 and if he makes that shot, $170,000.00 for a half court shot between quarters of a Boston

Celtics basketball game. Brian practiced for a week at a local community college and elementary school for the amazing opportunity. It was so fun watching Brian and Colin on the court of TD Banknorth Garden with a sold out crowd of fans ready to shoot the 3-pointer. The crowd hushed. Every fan was going to receive $10.00 if he made the shot. The professional basketball players and coaches turned to watch. Brian's image was on the Teletron. The lights dimmed. Brian took a deep breath. He lofted the ball in the perfect arch towards the basket and the ball hit the back of the rim and bounced off to the side. Damn icebergs!

Life cannot simply be an ongoing series of random events. Too many people wallow in their own misery. They feel trapped in ruts blaming the universe for their demise. Take charge of your own destiny. Life has too many icebergs without aiming at them. Vision without effort is fantasy. Effort without vision is drudgery. Have you ever dreamed of doing something that was really important to you? Was it enough to have this goal or was something else missing? Is it enough to simply have a goal or a life ambition? Many of us know what we want to achieve. It is easy to have an intention, an objective, or a star worth reaching. We all have personal and professional fantasies. Everyone wants to win the lottery, but wanting to win the lottery without buying a ticket is simply a fun fantasy. Actually buying a ticket is the only way that winning the lottery would ever become a reality. Obviously, winning the lottery is a long shot at best. However, as remote a possibility as winning the lottery may be, it is absolutely impossible without purchasing a ticket. Brian would not have had a chance of winning $170,000.00 for making two basketball shots unless he entered the contest. Whether your chances are 2:1, 10:1 or 1,000,000:1, remember that there is a 1. If you take enough measured risks, avoid making the same mistakes over and over again and keep trying, at some point the odds will work in your favor. I am convinced that some people are afraid to be happy. It takes little effort to be miserable. In fact, I am sure that there are some people who are not happy unless they are miserable. There are enough icebergs out there. Take some chances, navigate carefully, and maybe someday your ship will come in. It is not enough to simply have a fantasy. It must be followed with a plan or an action step. On the other hand, staying busy without an actual plan or a goal will not only result in little accomplishment, it will be tiresome and drudgery. Working at a job that you dislike will simply put you in a rut. However, doing a job search, generating a new resume, or taking a new course could take you out of the rut and into the groove that you seek. Take some time. Fantasize and then set up a first step that will actually begin the road to your dream. It will be amazing how easy next steps become when you get caught up in the momentum of your own energy.

Guillaume Apollinaire, innovator of French poetry, is best known for being accused of stealing the Mona Lisa. Among his many writings written before and during World War I, Apollinaire wrote a very simple poem that clarifies for me the complex issues of leadership, change, and risk. Apollinaire wrote,

"Come to the edge."
"We can't. We are afraid."
"Come to the edge."
"We can't. We will fall."
"Come to the edge."
And they came.
And he pushed them.
…And they flew.

Chapter 25: Final Thoughts

One day I was playing football in Colin's room on the floor with Colin and Makayla. Karen was sitting on the floor folding laundry as we played. I noticed on Colin's bed a good deal of money scattered on top of his bed. There were assorted bills and a large array of quarters, dimes, nickels, and pennies randomly scattered in no apparent pattern. Several coins were on the verge of falling off the bed and onto the floor. Out of curiosity, I asked Colin why was there so much money on his bed. He responded by saying, "I'm saving the money so I can buy something nice." I suggested to Colin that he consider putting the money into a piggy bank or into any other container so that he would not lose any of his savings. He agreed that Grampa had a good idea. I then took one of the pennies and held it up. I asked Colin what could he do with one penny. Colin replied, without hesitation, "Oh Grampa, I use the pennies to make wishes." I followed with, "Well, Colin, what would you wish with this penny?" He took the penny and immediately said, "I would wish that Grampa would stay forever." Karen and I looked at each other, our eyes welled up and I returned to continue playing football with two little angels.

I have much to do with the rest of my life. I read <u>Brown Bear,</u> <u>Brown Bear, What do You See?</u> by Bill Martin Jr. and Eric Carle to Makayla's preschool class. In addition, I read <u>A Picture for</u> <u>Harold's Room</u>, by Crockett Johnson, <u>Chicka Chicka 1 2 3</u>, by Bill Martin and Michael Sampson, and <u>I Wish I Had Duck Feet</u> , by Theo LeSieg to Colin's first grade class. Colin was so proud sitting next to me as his classmates sat on the floor listening to Grampa read the three books. When Harold described drawing an airplane, Colin leaned over to me and whispered, "Grampa, tell them that you fly airplanes." I have already started doing solo babysitting with Tyler. I am particularly proud of this because Tyler is still being nursed. However, give Grampa a bottle of breast milk and a microwave, and Grampa can do anything. I babysit for Noah and I am amazed at how much he is thriving. He is huge. Jeffrey has said to me how wonderful it would be when he is talking, walking, and having his own personality. I reassured Jeff that he will be doing those things before he knows it. I asked Jeff not to wish away one moment. Just enjoy that little boy every day. I do not fear getting older. I have so much to look forward to. In many ways, I feel as if my ship has already come in. Life does bring its challenges. There will be more icebergs to avoid. I may, in fact, hit a few of them, but I am not going to sink. I will continue to take measured chances. I have never been so busy in my life, yet ironically, I have never had so little stress. Perhaps for those of us who are Type A, it may be more stressful to wake up in the morning with nothing to do than it would be to wake up with a full schedule. For me, I am just glad to wake up. We have all heard the stories of busy people retiring after a long and healthy life, only to die within months after retiring.

When I die, my gravestone will not say that I was a principal, school superintendent, or a public speaker. It will not list my possessions or cite my 1040's documenting my annual income. None of my college degrees will be listed. It will not matter if I graduated with honors or squeaked by on academic probation. My gravestone will say that I was a beloved son, a Daddy, a Grampa and, if I navigate well enough, perhaps even a Great Grampa. In any case, note what those words are engraved on. They will remain forever on stone, long after resumes, college transcripts, tax returns, and bank accounts turn into faded yellow parchment. The most important things in life are not things. Nobody will stand in front of my grave and wonder how many bedrooms were in my house. Nobody regrets in the dwindling hours of his life that he had not worked longer hours. We will all be measured in terms of how many lives we touched. I recently gave a keynote address at an upper Cape Cod preschool teachers' conference. At the end of my speech, an animated woman came up to me and excitedly informed me that she was Colin's preschool teacher. I was so delighted and I told her that Colin adores her. Without hesitation, she responded by saying, "I know." Each year in her class, she gives the children an interesting exercise. She asks the children four questions. She then writes down the children's answers and sends the children home with the questionnaire.

Here are the questions and answers on Colin's paper.

1. What is your favorite color? Colin said, "<u>Blue</u>."
2. What is your favorite animal? Colin said, "<u>Hippopotamus</u>."
3. What is your favorite food? Colin said, "<u>Melon</u>."
4. What is your favorite thing to do? Colin said, "<u>Play with Grampa</u>."

How does one stay motivated on the Titanic? Despite rough seas, icebergs and long journeys, I believe in my heart that we all finds ways to survive, indeed thrive, if we choose to do so. I wake up every day motivated, not to just stay alive, but to live.

A little boy made a wish on an old tarnished Lincoln penny, and I am going to do everything in my power to make that wish come true.